© 1996 Lunwerg Editores, S.A.
© 1996 Publio López Mondejár
© text: Joaquín Vidal
© 1996 the photographers
© photography: Ramón Masats
Original title: Fotografía y Sociedad en La España de Franco

Idea, Design and Realization: Lunwerg Editores, S.A.

Copyright © 1999 for this English edition
Könemann Verlagsgesellschaft mbH
Bonner Str. 126, D-50968 Cologne

Translated by Lucilla Watson
Edited and typeset by Book Creation Services Ltd
Project co-ordinator: Tami Rex

Printing and Binding: Mateu Cromo, Madrid

Printed in Spain

ISBN: 3-8290-2223-9

10 9 8 7 6 5 4 3 2 1

PHOTOGRAPHY IN
FRANCO'S SPAIN

Publio López Mondéjar

KÖNEMANN

CONTENTS

HERMES PATO. Beggar. Madrid, October 1940. (Efe Archive)

A REFLECTION OF LIFE IN BLACK AND WHITE

Antonio Muñoz Molina

There is a spirit of the age and of events that is uniquely contained in the medium of photographs. Without that spirit, a particular kind of experience or of memory would not exist; and it is not to be found in any other artistic medium. In a famous diatribe, Baudelaire accused photography of invading and corroding memory because, providing an exact record of faces, places, and events, it invaded a territory that belonged to memory. It is curious that Baudelaire's objection is the very same that Plato leveled against Socrates on the subject of writing: that through their very existence, images and the written word, being devised to record facts, paradoxically led to the atrophy of memory.

I do not know, now, whether all that is true, whether photography has changed or weakened my own powers of memory: what I do know is that, for me, the intensity of true time, of real people, of city streets, is never more effectively captured than through black and white photography, in this alchemy of optics, chemistry and light that never ceases to astonish me and that always seems to be midway between witchcraft and poetry, between pure craftsmanship and the most improbable chance.

It is through photographs that, as children, we first gain an intuition that time has another dimension that goes back far into the past, that faces and people's ages are not permanent, that before we came into the world there existed people who have died. My clearest childhood memories are not memories of people and places but of photographs. I recall the busts of my mother's grandparents, rigid and dressed as if in mourning, in a large wooden-framed photograph that hung above a chest, and how this piece of furniture, with its deep drawers that were faintly out of bounds, had something funerary about it, so that the photograph, so high up on the wall that children gazed up at it from below, filled me with even greater foreboding.

Seen at close range, those photographs had the hard consistency of cardboard and were a pale brown color, a little faded round the edges, in their tinted backgrounds, and in the outlines of a necktie or lapel of a jacket that had visibly been retouched by hand—a mourning jacket like those in which the dead were so frequently seen to be dressed in photographs.

Baudelaire, if I think specifically of my own experience, was right about one thing: my memory is full of photographs. But my memory would not be purer if those photographs had never existed, if they had not attracted me from the time that I was a child, when I would search for them in the bottom of drawers or inside those tins my mother used for storing them in.

If it were not for those photographs, my memory would be much the poorer and it would also be a lesser memory since, before I reached the age of reason, I would not have sensed the poetry and enigma of the time span of human lives. Each photograph that I examined was an interrogation, a potential history of someone whom I did not know but who was very relevant to me, who had once lived in the same house that I now lived in, at a time before I was born or at the time of my earliest memories. There was a young man, with very striking looks and a wide, bronzed face, dressed in military uniform—albeit the type of uniform that one might see in the movies—with a white waistband and a plumed hat, his elbow resting on one of those plinths that often appear in old photographs: he was an uncle of my mother's whom not even she had known, a dead man from the distant past who had survived for three years in the African war and who died of pneumonia within a few weeks of his return.

That photograph was the testimony of his youth cut short by arbitrary ill luck; it was the repository of the grief of his sister, my grandmother, who years later still thought about him and who frequently looked at the photograph and said: "What a handsome man my brother was. How fine he was."

For her, too, the memory of her dead brother was set forever in that face in the photograph. And she herself, from whom I learnt so many things and about whom I remember so very much, is becoming blurred in my memory; I keep her memory alive through the photographs that document her life, such as the picture of her on her wedding day in 1923, the picture of her with me when I was four or five years old, and, her appearance in the final color photographs, as an elderly woman, her hair always slightly unkempt, wearing the glasses that never arrested the onset of blindness, wearing a thick blue wrap drawn around her shoulders.

No other art form speaks to me so powerfully from the most tender and intimate part of my being as does photography. It speaks to me of myself and of the world, of my own past and that which I share with others, and the past that I remember without having lived it. For me, photography has always had a dual quality, being on the one hand a skilled trade and on the other something that has about it a touch of witchcraft and magical phantasmagoria. Even today, however, there are those who choose to disdain it, so as to prevent it from so much as gaining a foothold in the margins of reality and so as to keep it scrupulously free of the slightest documentary value, of the smallest tremor of human experience.

The photographer who looks at the world round about him, who seeks in people's faces and in the reality of events the tremor of a revelation, will be accused by those authorities and commentators of sensationalism; these narrow-minded people want to make of photography what they have made of almost all the arts over the last few decades: an isolated realm from which the world is debarred, an exclusive club, a sector infiltrated with its own jargon and, like everything else, hermetically self-contained. For professional photographers, as for those who work professionally in any other field, what is most important is not the photographs themselves: it is the knowledge that they share a certain privilege that is not open to the majority of people—who are spared the unpleasant accretions of reality.

Fortunately, no art form is as pure as the conceited puritanism of the experts requires. Painting, fiction, music, the movies are all made up of a host of different elements, of experiences and dreams, of the sublime and the vulgar, of the most trivial and the most deeply significant. What Pío Baroja said about the novel or the movies can also be said about photography: that it is a great sack into which everything falls, into which in a particular way life and time, the exact form of the present that, no longer existing, becomes part of the remote past, so that, as Antonio Machado has it, the present is always with us. There are people who, not knowing any other way to earn their living, spend their time classifying and subdividing things, drawing distinctions between the art photographer and the photojournalist, between art and craftsmanship, between solid documents and pure invention. All this is so much nonsense. A great photograph is both a literal testimony and a piece of pure creativity. In 1995, one of the photographs in a magnificent exhibition of the work

of Gervasio, on the theme of the siege of Sarajevo, was of an old man wrapped up in old winter clothes and holding up a spoon to the light of a candle: that photograph expressed all the horror of the war, the pathos of hunger, and the bitterness of helpless old age, but at the same time there was a density in the shadows and a dignity in the figure of the old man that made me think of the darkly shadowed portraits of Rembrandt.

Perhaps that is what we find so fascinating about the work of professional photographers: the interplay of beauty and truth, of perfection and unsightliness, of the quotidian and the mysterious. The character that I once invented as a protagonist in a novel that I wrote was that of a provincial photographer, a wedding photographer and snapper of military recruits, who kept all the photographs that had ever been taken in his studio in the course of the century, storing them in a chest unsorted, without valuing some above others, simply keeping them all hidden away, consigned to a depository of stationary time and lost faces.

Years after that novel was published, I received a consignment of photographs that had been unearthed by Publio López Mondéjar, and in them I found a collection that was every bit as extensive as the hoard put away by my fictional portrait photographer, a meticulously detailed record of Spanish lives and photographs that went back further than those pictures of my grandparents in their youth that had so captivated me as a child.

Single-handedly, for no reason other than his great interest in photographs, Publio López Mondéjar spent years investigating provincial studios, seeking out the testimony of anonymous photographers and of the equally nameless people that had been their subjects. Finally, when he had gathered them all together and sorted them into different volumes, the end result of his labors had become a unique encyclopedia of the ghosts of dead people, a memory bank of all the lives, land-scapes, trades, sufferings and gazes that would otherwise have been consigned to oblivion; everything that would have been swept from the face of the earth were it not for these photographs, and for the passion that drove Publio López Mondéjar on in his researches.

There was method to this passion: Publio López Mondéjar wanted to compile a history of Spanish life, a series of episodes in the life of the nation in black and white like those documenting the last years of the Spanish monarchy, the Republic, and the Civil War that had been taken by Alfonso. That dynamic photo-journalist in a sharp suit, trilby, and round glasses treated his photographic subjects, whether Abd el-Krim or Niceto Alcalá Zamora, in exactly the same way, and showed an absolute mastery of tenebrism in that final and tragically sad picture of the Civil War in which Julián Besteiro makes a radio broadcast under the shadow of his guard, Colonel Casado.

Publio López Mondéjar shows his collections of photographs with the enthusiasm of an avaricious multimillionaire: on tables, on the floor, over the arms of chairs in the lounge of his house, he has spread out for me the images that make up the latest of his historical instalments, from Franco's victory in 1939 to the tremulous celebrations of freedom in 1977. Those photographs that he lay out before me rekindled in me the feeling that I had when I looked at photographs of my forebears in their youth and of my parents; through them I have traveled right back to my earliest memories, to the things that I knew not because I was told about them or because I have seen them in photographs and in the movies but because I have witnessed them, because a long time ago my childlike eyes told me about them.

Here are the darkened faces, the tattered shoes of poverty, the horror of uniforms and of the shaven heads of prisoners, the mournful drape of a priest's soutane, the paving stones of streets, of fists thrust high in the fascist sign of the victors, the crucifixes, and the portraits of Franco and José Antonio that I saw in school, the sinister darkness and ingrained poverty of a defeated country not so much arrested in time as forcibly pushed back into the past, poisoned anew by fear and religion, by malnutrition and political obscurantism. I recognize those faces, those whitewashed walls, those rays of light from a bygone age, but I also sense, in a way that only photography explains, the slow evolution of the times, the change from one world to another, which is all the more stirring when one has lived in both.

Anonymous photographers have a ready instinct for formal subtleties, for the suggestion of poetry through the tough exterior of the world that they portray: corres-pondingly, photographers who put their name to their work, such as Ontañón and Cualladó, seek an effect of the utmost seriousness that puts us in mind of the gravitas achieved by the portrait photographers whose clients were the brides and grooms of our parents' generation. In this world of ghosts, inhabited by young girls of the early 1960s who are the subject of coarse amorous advances made in the middle of the street by a delinquent youth with slicked-down hair, suddenly appears the noble and solitary figure of Pío Baroja, who in hat and coat strolls beneath the trees of El Retiro, on a winter's morning that dawned on a day before I was born and that I nevertheless seem to remember.

As the great wind of change cuts a swathe through the time encapsulated by these photographs, swastika flags fade away, ceding center stage to the recaptured flags of the 1970s: the picture of a young woman standing naked on the statues of Daoíz and Velarde is in itself a signal of triumph, an allegorical apparition as vibrant as that of the bare-breasted woman who leads the populace to the barricades in Delacroix's *Liberty Leading the People*.

This is part of our experience, and that of those now dead, and it will be with the very same anonymous, melancholic expressions that we will be seen when people look at photographs of our own present. The camera obscura, the *chambre claire* (camera clara) of Roland Barthes, the room lit up with photographs, is a permanent museum, a space for living, the house and the great library of photographs which Publio López Mondéjar personally curated. But if photographs have the power to move us so, it is for a deeper reason: only they allow us the illusion of going back to the inaccessible time that preceded our own existence, those days when our parents were young.

A.M.M.

PREFACE AND ACKNOWLEDGMENTS

This book is the third volume in a publishing project that began 15 years ago with the idea of re-creating a picture of a Spain that is no more, through the seeds of memory that photography shows. In the puzzling absence of any comprehensive works on the subject, the aim was also to compile a history of photography in Spain from its earliest beginnings up to the eve of the 21st century, and its interrelation with the social, political, and cultural life of the country.

As with the earlier volumes, the images selected for this book have been chosen on the basis of their ability to tell a story, to record historical fact, and to reflect the past, for their evocative force and their power to snatch time from oblivion. These pictures not only express the views of those who took them; they are also statements of the reality that they record. More than a mere history of photography, this book aims to chronicle, from a human point of view, 40 years of life in Spain, from the end of the Civil War to the eve of the transition to democracy. It is a chronicle made up of the photographs that I have found most arresting, captivating, or moving. I could never have made this selection without the generous cooperation of people who, throughout the years, gave me their assistance, their time, and their friendship.

To the following, I should like to extend my sincere thanks: J. Antonio Pérez Millán, Basilio Martín Patino, Maite Conesa, Carlos Zardoya, Mateo Gamón, Francisco Rodríguez, Salvador Martínez, Mariano Bombín, Pablo Montejano, Josep Gol, Andreu Catalá, Xosé Luis Cabo, Manuel Sendón, Josep Cruañas, Manuel López Rodríguez, Rosario Martínez Rochina, Lola Garrido, Mercedes Heredero, Ana Muller, Manuel Lafuente Caloto, Santiago Bernal, María Teresa Gutiérrez Barranco, Gregorio Merino, Carmelo Tartón, Maite Muñoz, José Gálvez, Carlos Cánovas, and so many others whom I have unintentionally overlooked; Juan Manuel Castro Prieto and Mario Parralejo, who so skillfully made prints of the photographs and to whom I am indebted for their valuable suggestions and advice; Carlos Ortega, who shared with me the task of selecting and ordering the photographs that were to make up the exhibition for which this book serves as the catalog; Antonio Muñoz Molina, for having written the foreword; Josep María Ribas Prous, whose generosity was overwhelming; Carlos and Consuelo, who read the text; Luis Escobar, Mari Paz Elícegui, Juani and Carmen Vielba, Susi Pacheco, Carmen Botán, Ramón Vallvé, Federico Vélez, José Cartagena, Luis Pérez de León, Luzzi Wolgensinger, Elías and Juan Carlos Dolcet, José Aguayo, Miguel Quintas, and Lidia Anoz, who had the wisdom to preserve their family archives and who made them available to me; Catalá Roca, Jean Dieuzaide, Jean Mohr, and Marc Riboud, who through their generous assistance made my work easier; Carlos Cánovas, Martín García, Ribas Prous, Manel Serra, and Javier Berasaluce for their valuable contribution and excellent printing of the photographs by Arina, Arque, Maspons, Miserachs, Catany, Cuadrada, Massó, Olivé, Terré, and Manel Armengol; Paola Concepción, who continually gave me her valuable assistance; Carlos Pérez Siquier, Gonzalo Juanes, Ramón Masats, Alberto Schommer, Leopoldo Pomés, Eugenio Forcano, Paco Gómez, Oriol Maspons, Xavier Miserachs, Gerardo Vielba, Gabriel Cualladó, and Paco Ontañon, who made such a momentous contribution to the rebirth of Spanish photography and who did so much to help me gain an insight into photography in the 1950s and 1960s. I would like to single out for special mention Gerardo Vielba, whose words never failed to give me encouragement.

Finally, I would like to extend particular acknowledgment to all photographers, regardless of whether their work appears in this selection. They are the real authors of this book, whose aim it is to record their work through years dogged by so many difficulties and by such hardship and deprivation.

Publio López Mondéjar
Casasimarro, March 1996

11

FOR CONSUELO AND LUCÍA

The magazine *Fotos*, 15 April 1939 issue.

On that day, 1 April 1939, the rebel troops that had gathered against the Republican government realized their ultimate military objectives, inaugurating a regime midway between fascism and the military and religious dictatorship that Manuel Azaña, the Republican statesman, had predicted. With military victory a political system was implanted in Spain that, in the rhetorical hyperbole of the period, was "nationalist, authoritarian, unitarian, ethical, missionary, and imperial." The reality of that Spain, dominated by the financial, political, and religious factions that made up the so-called "nationalist" forces, has been eloquently described by Dionisio Ridruejo: "The 1940s," wrote this Falangist intellectual, "were, for most of the population, years of pain, humiliation, hunger, and fear in a climate of safe-conducts for traveling and ration cards to obtain miserable rations. For the small, deeply vulgarized class of mandarins who respected no one and for rich speculators, they were years of wild euphoria." These were also years of repression, penance, and terror.

In the summer of 1939, there were 29 working prisons in Madrid where more than 100,000 prisoners were crowded together. Every morning in the courts of Las Salesas, five very brief Councils of War were held, in which 300 to 400 defendants were summarily tried and condemned. A similar process went on in every major city in the country, in which as many as 150 concentration camps were hastily put up. Count Ciano, who then visited Spain, noted in his memoirs: "A large number of executions by firing squad were then taking place. In Madrid alone there were 200 to 250 a day, in Barcelona 150, and in Seville 80." In December 1939 the Ministry of Justice itself officially recognized the existence of 271,000 political prisoners, and up until 1951 a total of 164,642 "violent deaths." "The end of the conflict," wrote García de Cortázar y González Vesga, "did not result in peace for the people of Spain, it only gave them a political order. Hundreds of people found themselves forced to watch their conduct and change their lives drastically in accordance with the political and social demands of the new state. Thousands more fell victim to the firing squads. Those who, working clandestinely, had been members of defeated political organizations, suffered permanent social proscription."[1] In his desire to keep alive the spirit of cruelty that made possible social confrontation, General Franco did not lift the state of war until 1948, and the military tribunals continued their program of repression for almost 40 years.

In that situation, the value of the peseta fell to half what it had been in 1936. In 1940 the national income had shrunk to its 1914 level, while per capita income had descended to the values of the 19th century. By 1950, with peasants making up 48.8 percent of the country's economically active population, Spain continued to be a typical agrarian and preindustrial country. While the working population had shrunk by more than half a million, new jobs went to the "ex-combatants" of the victorious faction, and the army maintained 500,000 officers and soldiers on its payroll. Until 1951, Spain was in the grip of autocracy, economic stagnation, and inflation. Franco's Spain became inward-looking, condemning Spaniards to a long and impoverishing period of international isolation. In March 1946, the French government closed its frontier with Spain. Weeks later the governments of the United States, Great Britain, and France issued a statement in which they stated that "for as long as General Franco continues to govern Spain, the Spanish people cannot expect full and cordial relations with those nations of the world who, through their combined efforts, have defeated German Nazism and Italian Fascism, both of which helped the present Spanish regime into power and supported it."

In the domain of culture, the situation in Spain was turning into something very much like so much uncultivated land, given that the authorities who had been in charge of keeping culture alive now showed nothing more than an evident indifference. Millán Astray's famous slogan, "Death to the intelligentsia," was nothing more than a local variant of Goebbels's

JOSÉ SERRANO. Nationalist troops enter a "liberated" village in Andalusia. (Serrano Archive, Hemeroteca Municipal de Sevilla)

statement: "When I hear the word culture I reach for my gun." With the military victory, cultural life in Spain was violently curtailed; most writers, artists, musicians, and scientists went into exile; others were imprisoned or purged, or found themselves forced to go underground, leading a semiclandestine existence. In any case, their work was persecuted and banned, and censorship was not lifted until the very last days of the regime.

For obvious reasons, social conditions in Spain at that time were not in the smallest way reflected in art or literature, nor of course in photography. Photography, which openly espoused the neoclassical canons of the 1940s, was steeped in a formulaic, old-fashioned, and jingoistic sentimentality. Spain—a great and unified country, albeit not free—was the recurring theme of the old, academic style of photography, by contrast to the picture of profound depression and poverty that even the regime's loudest propagandists could not hide. Pictorialism was the photographic style that most closely matched the new government's triumphalist and myth-making spirit, and the dictatorship's moral and artistic poverty. Cultural nationalism espoused the esthetic ideas that

had driven this movement, so that folklorism and the extolling of race, tradition, and a now imperial past pervaded the work of the best-known photographic "artists" of the postwar years. This situation was not to change until the end of that period of dictatorship.

IN THE SERVICE OF EMPIRE

Spanish neopictorialism was the apotheosis of the old photographic impressionism, whose main aim had been none other than to raise photography to the status of the fine arts. The excessively allegorical style of early pictorialism was abandoned in favor of an emphatically more painterly and ostensibly more documentary style, which was seen as a vehicle for the glorification of Spanish national dress, customs, and traditions, and the landscape of Spain. This was an obviously idealized style of photography, in which the esthetic values of the remaining aristocracy were substituted for those of the new, powerful middle class. Alongside the best and most vigorous style photography of the period, that of Alfred Stieglitz, Eugène Atget, Paul Strand, Edward Weston, and

José Ortiz Echagüe—the last pictorialist, as Daniel Masclet described him—was doubtless the most distinguished exponent of this photographic style. His technical mastery of the effects of light and shade, his powerful photographic vision, and his great compositional genius, perfectly equipped him for this style of photography, which was both interpretative and imbued with "eternal values," values all keenly endorsed by Prensa y Propaganda (Press and Propaganda). Thus was Echagüe long recognized as the most emblematic photographer of the new Spain, a Spain where, according to Giménez Caballero, the artist should also be a great soldier and a great Spaniard.

In the midst of this rhetorical apotheosis, Ortiz Echagüe completed his monumental trilogy, which began with *España, tipos y trajes* (1933, Spain, people and dress) and *España, pueblos y paisajes* (1938, Spain, villages and landscapes). *España mística* (Mystic Spain) appeared in 1943, and *Castillos y alcázares* (Castles and palaces) in 1956. With these two latter works, Echagüe completed his personal re-creation of a Spain that, in keeping with the ideology of the period, he wanted to be mystical and warlike, one great unified country purged of heretics, separatists, and masons. As J. Salaverría pointed out, his photographs bear all the marks of "artistic and patriotic fervor." In this context, he did not scruple to stage-manage themes and idealize people and places, even going so far as to dress up his subjects in clothes especially obtained for the shot. Just as he had done in the earlier *Sermón de aldea* (1903, Sermon in a hamlet) or *Lino de Orio* (1923, Orio flax), many of his shots were staged. This is evidenced in the famous *Beso al Prior* (1944, Kissing the prior's hand), which, as Echagüe himself acknowledged, is an "over-arranged" photograph. His deeply-felt religious fervor and his submission to a style of photography that was predetermined by that of painting drove Echagüe not only to set up the shot but also to manipulate the image; thus he thought nothing of altering the bare interior of the prior's cell, bringing a note of pomposity with the serene clouds that appear in the finished version.

Echagüe went on working until 1973, and his granitic, schematic work continued essentially unchanged, although in his final years it became more synthetic and "photographic." "The ultraconservative character of his work," wrote José Horna, "which has remained immovable over 70 years, was not confined to photographic technique but also applied to an underlying theme, so that the nationalism–catholicism and millenarianism of an eternal Spain impregnated the subject-matter and the composition of every photograph he took…. [His works] unequivocally express a vision of the country rooted in

the revolution brought about by the avant-garde between the wars, Spanish neopictorialism was a kind of photographic *género chico* (light theatrical work), depicting a crude, grandiloquent, and theatrical Spain.[2]

In the climate of patriotic glorification that followed in the wake of the military victory of 1939, art was seen as something merely ceremonial, at the service of the state and the empire; it was conventional and reverential. The esthetic of Franco's dictatorship, defined by Giménez Caballero, José María Pemán, Eugenio Montes, García Valdecasas, or Laín Entralgo, was a confused dough of rhetoric that bore a close relation to the values of prewar neopictorialism and which centered around the nation's greatness and unity, the glorification of the past, of tradition and of a baroque, rusty Catholicism.

"Art," announced the Falangist periodical *Jerarquía*, "needs a metaphysic to live; and if in place of a metaphysic it is given a theology, great will be its struggle to flourish."[3] This is not to imply that the cultural doctrine of Franco's dictatorship was in line with this movement's esthetic, whose longevity can only be understood in terms of the conspicuous support given to it by the highest ranks of the new regime.

the most immovable opposition to change and in the negation of any trace of modernity. For Echagüe the only Spain that existed was that of bell towers and mourning, castles and crucifixes, ancient nobility and suits of armor; of order and unity cloaked in the patriotic celebration of local customs."[4]

Such was the stature of this unique and major figure that his work effectively overshadowed that of all the other neopictorialist photographers of the time, who although they were less driven by ideology, continued to mine the vein of the old picturesque folklorism in overly-confected compositions. But among them were some who had already chosen a different path, such as José Tinoco, Francisco Andrada, Joaquín Plá Janini, Eduardo Susanna, the Count of Ventosa, Antonio Arissa, Casals Ariet, Mora Carbonell, Miguel Goicoechea, Antoni Campañá (who soon sought new directions in sports photography), the Marquess of Santa María del Villar, Carlos Gutiérrez, and Joaquín Gil Marraco. These photographers were mostly anchored in a decorative, make-believe preciocity that was very much in line with the wishes of a regime that was trying to draw a veil over the harsh reality of the country through an art—and photography was by no means exempt—that was being made to serve a ceremonial and dissimulating role. In this sense, neopictorialism was both the product of the dictatorship and the national photographic contribution to the regime.

Joaquín Plá Janini, who with Ortiz Echagüe most strongly influenced Spanish photographers of the period, deserves special mention. He most conspicuously upheld the painterly style of photography, maintained the most tenacious resistance against new currents in photography, and most strongly championed the return to true "art" photography, which for him was none other than painterly photography. "Painterly processes," he wrote in 1940, "which have almost completely been pushed to one side, are the only means of bringing out a photographer's artistic taste and capability ... only [transport] can translate an image to paper such as that used by draftsmen and etchers, removing what is unpleasant about photography to convert it into an imitation of a good drawing or etching."[5] If he had ever felt the call of change in his working habits that might lead him to try out new forms and make purely visual experiments, Plá Janini soon returned to the old ways, with their threadbare, formally academicist, and conceptually conservative esthetic. In these final years he was unable to avoid the documentalist impulse, which is present in such works as *Bajo los puentes* (1946) or in some exceptional bromide in which he shows a certain capacity for reportage.

The influence of Plá Janini, Ortiz Echagüe, Tinoco, Andrada, and Susanna was decisive for the survival of the painterly style of photography in Spain in the 1940s and into the early 1950s. Exponents of this style included Inocencio Smith de las Heras, the Marquess of Urrecha, Ramón Alsius y Malagelada, Sigfrido Koch Bengoechea, Josep and Manuel Closa, Casals Ariet, Pau Barceló, Pere Sender, Martín Burillo, J. Marías Pascual, Federico Ferrando, José A. Lassala, and many prominent members of the photographic associations of the time whose work was exploited by the new cultural authorities through the Ministry of Press and Propaganda's Department of Plastic Arts. This department, as well as censuring works of art, took on the organization of national photographic exhibitions, which fell under the aegis of the photographic division, run by Augusto Vallmitjana, who had close links with the Agrupación Fotográfica de Cataluña.

The exhibitions (Salones Nacionales de la Fotografía), together with the photographic societies and new specialist magazines, strongly influenced the work of the new generation of painterly photographers, which was

Two versions of *Kissing the prior's hand* (1944) by ORTIZ ECHAGÜE. (Ortiz Echagüe Bequest, University of Navarre)

indebted to a folklorism that stressed the values of a "virile" Spain by contrast to an "industrial and liberal Europe." "What Spain is envied for," wrote Eugenio Montes in 1953, "is its manliness. What the technical-minded, industrial, liberal, capitalist, and socialist man cannot forgive the Spaniard is that he is simply more manly." In their work, the new Spanish painterly photographers celebrated the peace, joy, honor, and "harmony without anxiety" of Spanish rural and peasant life, an attitude encouraged by such theorists as Eduardo Aunós, conspicuous champion of photography with a soul and conscious of its "spiritual mission."[6]

This was something that remained as a leitmotif in the work of the most typical exponents of the movement, among them José Loygorry, J. Domingo Bisbal, Manuel Cuadrada, Ramón Godó, Miguel Tubáu, Luis Paz, Tomás de Arcillona, Sierra Calvo, Francisco P. de Ponti, the Marquess of Aledo, the Marquess of Loriana, Diego Gálvez, Rafael Gómez Teruel, A. Forradana Coll, Josep Massó, Pere Sender, José Veiga Roel, and Núñez Larraz. Some of them—Pere Sender, Veiga Roel, Loygorry, Massó, and Núñez Larraz—acted as a bridge with the kind of

documentary realism practised by the next generation. The creative schizophrenia that these photographers experienced was eloquently expressed by Veiga Roel at the exhibition of Otto Steinert's work in Vigo in 1961: "I am not yet sufficiently well informed to declare myself in favor of one or other of these styles (the classic or the 'modern'), especially when I am persuaded that what is old and outmoded is in need of an urgent, cataclysmic revolution, and what is presented to us as new does not seem to me like a sincere and spontaneous manifestation of art."[7]

Veiga Roel was honestly describing the conflict experienced by many photographers, rooted as they were in endemic academism but endowed with sufficient creativity to latch onto the currents of change that were then beginning to blow through the country. Some of Veiga Roel's last works, and he was one of the most emblematic and best-known exhibitors of his time, anticipate that new documentary realism, whose beginnings could just be discerned in certain images by Miguel Goicoechea, Plá Janini, José Tinoco, and Ortiz Echagüe, who always denied with "naïve vehemence" that he was a pictorialist photographer.

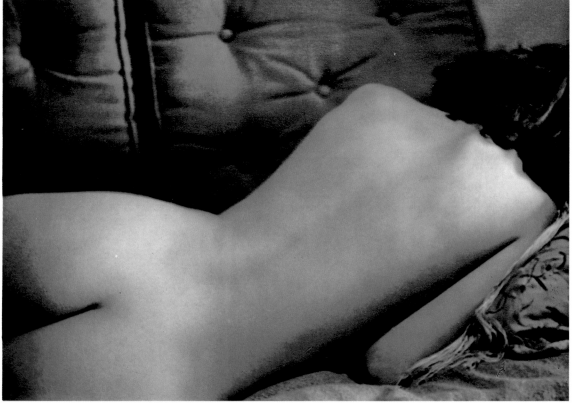

NICOLÁS MULLER. Female nude. 1949. (Muller Archive)

OTHO LLOYD. *Rest. Study of shoulders*. 1946. (Salvador Martínez Collection)

RAMÓN BARGUÉS. Nude.
(*Sombras* yearbook, 1948)

JOSEP MARÍA RIBAS PROUS.
Nude. c. 1970.
(Photographer's collection)

top-notch publications, whose higher price put them out of the reach of the great mass of the people."[8]

So stifling did censorship become that the nude was permanently banned from exhibitions and competitions until well into the 1960s. As a result, photographers avoided this subject until the beginning of the transition to democracy, and it was very rare to come across photographs of nudes in the 1940s and 1950s, except in the commendable work of Otho Lloyd and Nicolás Muller, who had received their training outside Spain. It was not until 1958 that Ramón Bargués' nudes saw the light of day, published in the Afal yearbook of 1958, after a determined struggle with the government. Feeble attempts at the genre were made by Leopoldo Pomés, Oriol Maspons, Colita, and César Malet in the 1960s, and by Josep María Ribas Prous, Gonzalo Vinagre, the Yeti, Jorge Rueda, Francisco Vila Masip, Jeroni Vives, Vilalta Sensada, Luis Pérez Mínguez, Alberto Schommer, the brothers Eguiguren, J. M. Oriola, César Lucas, and Joan Salvadó in the 1970s. However, the nude was never more than a semi-underground genre that was never very prominent in Spanish photography during the Franco years. A frequent contributor to *Arte Fotográfica* gave a personal explanation for this in 1967: "We well knew that it was timidity, the absence of precedent, as much as fear of being labeled wimps, the problem of prejudice, the specter of censorship, and the thought of being debarred from taking part in exhibitions that inhibited any initiative in this direction." "It is advisable," wrote Juan Domingo Bisbal, in the June 1973 issue of *Arte Fotográfica*, "to keep a watch on the nude in photography, which should adhere to the strictest moral guidelines." So relentlessly persecuted was the nude during the Nationalist–Catholic years that, as Ribas Prous recently stated, this genre became for the members of his generation a kind of disobedience in the face of the dictatorship's cultural and moral oppression. Probably for this reason, in the years of the transition to democracy, a rough and sometimes aggressive style of nude photography developed, in reaction against the puritanism, the repression, and the censorship of the previous era.

However, this was not what most preoccupied the jealous guardians of the regime's moral and political orthodoxy, who were more interested in hiding and disguising the harsh reality of a country straining under dictatorship, rationing, and the black market. This was a task in which that celebrated style of photography played a far from insignificant role—a style of photography practised by the country's most prominent neo-pictorialists, and by the great legion of their followers and imitators.

The task of concealing, idealizing, and "poeticizing" reality undertaken by postwar "art" photography was completed by the distinguished work of those in charge of censorship, imposed by the authorities of the new regime so as to preserve the purity of the country's customs and traditions, and safeguard the moral and religious values of the glorious Nationalist Movement. From the time of the Serrano Law of 1938, publications, performances, and works of art of every kind were subject to censorship. Censoring photography fell to the Photographic Division of the Ministry of Press and Propaganda. In years when the Nationalist–Catholic orthodoxy was obsessive in its upholding of morality, censorship meant a severe clampdown on any minor infringement, quite apart from the total banishment of any publication that ran counter to the basic principles of the regime.

"The censors' severity when it came to artistic reproduction," recalled Alonso Tejada, "or to straightforward photographs of women in books, magazines, or newspapers was atrocious. The nude disappeared from the history of art, except in the really

THE DAWN OF REALITY

In the cultural wasteland of the postwar years, it was never going to be easy for Spanish photographers to move closer to the "modern" style of photography that some members of the younger generation were beginning to demand, whether it was expressionist, abstract, impressionist, or realist. "What should we see as the opposite of the concept of modern photography?" wondered José María Artero in 1956. "Simply, pictorial photography. Those are the fundamentally opposed elements: a style of photography that wants to be a bad imitation of the previous century's, as opposed to the photography of our time; photography that is vicarious, parasitic, and in the grip of shameless mimicry, as opposed to photography that is free, splendid, infinite."

But, at the height of the pictorialist revival, this "free and splendid" style looked to by those young photographers who were to play a leading part in the future renewal in Spanish photography was, with very few exceptions, discernible only in the work of popular photographers whose lack of pretentiousness preserved them from the artistic excesses of the time. By comparison with the artificiality, imitation, and what passed for originality in the work of so-called art photographers, their work, despite its obvious technical limitations, was uniquely capable of showing us a pale glimmer of the life of ordinary people as they went about their daily business. "With this kind of photography," wrote Alexandre Cirici in 1958, "countless technically flawed photographs have an extraordinary life, helping us to know the world and even to know ourselves. Over and over again, by contrast, we see competition photographs that are technically perfect but have no real meaning." "Those who safeguarded in their work the purity of photography," wrote Brassaï in 1932, "were photographers without artistic pretensions. They were the ones who first questioned the omnipotence of art, which exercised precedence in every aspect of reality."[9] In the simple and moving pictures of these photographers, the sitters are the only stars, the photographer limiting himself to a role of invisible creator, who works the miracle of preserving for the future the slice of life that passes before his camera lens.

Popular photographers kept alive the traditions of the old traveling photographers of the prewar years, who had to respond to the increasing demand of local people who, through portraits of family and neighbors, sought to rebuild the emotional geography of their familiar surroundings, now doubly devastated, not only as a result of illness or oblivion, but by imprisonment, exile, or death on unknown frontiers. In the climate of economic deprivation of those harsh years, it was only

ANONYMOUS. (Attributed to LUIS ESCOBAR.) Funeral of "los Caídos" (the Fallen Ones). Casasimarro, 1939. (Private collection)

through the work of traveling photographers that the profession survived, the latter in turn ensuring the survival of those unpretentious, simple images that are still to be found in old family albums or in our grandparents' chests and trunks.

"Fortunately," wrote Muñoz Molina, "photography has been a profession for most of its existence, and the photographer someone who sought to make an honest living through his work. A large painting or sculpture can only be viewed somewhere that has been specially arranged for it; a great photograph can speak to us in a museum display or under the spotlights of a gallery; but it can do so equally when we idly turn the pages of a newspaper, leaf through a magazine, or glance at a shop window, and also look through an album full of our parents' memories."[10]

RUFINO. Beggar. 1950. (Rufino Archive)

Together with this straightforward type of photography practised by those anonymous and forgotten professionals, there survived a type of popular reportage whose capacity to surprise or dazzle sprang from the simplicity of its authors. Despite the lack of means, deprivation, and improvisation, the images produced by the occasional press photographers of the time today constitute a moving testimony of a paralyzed country that was still recovering from the ravages of war. Through these pictures, photography, like a living evocation of the past and beyond its technical or artistic merits, presents us with its visual testimony of the way things were. Unlike official press photographers, these ordinary photographers have not the slightest interest in hiding the devastations of reality and, whenever circumstances allowed, they developed what was in effect the opposite of the kind of image called for by the offices of Press and Propaganda. In their work we find an unvarnished perception of Spain in the grip of the black market, hunger, repression, and ration cards.

PEDRO MENCHÓN. Unveiling of the monument to "los Caídos" (the Fallen Ones). Lorca, 1940. (Archivo Municipal de Lorca)

If they were not born of "silence, fear, and powerlessness," the forgotten and largely destroyed images of those photojournalists constitute a mirror that reflects the desolate landscape of defeat, the dark world of alienation and suffering: those orphanages filled with the heirs of misfortune, street beggars drawing their children to them as if they were chicks—frightened, broken people who suffered persecution in the name of justice, the dark maw of shelters, the legion of destitute people who stayed alive by frequenting the sordid refectories of the social centers, political prisoners forced to accept the liturgy of victory, the sad and solemn funerals of the fallen ones…. Even the photography then used to construct a hyperbolic picture of the Motherland is today—only half a century later—an implacable interrogation of those who produced it, and a real "negative of victory" that stands as testimony to precisely the opposite of what was shouted from the rooftops of officialdom.

Of the provincial photographers, some had begun their work some years previously, and among them were Luis Escobar, Gregorio Muñoz, Antonio Avilés, Fernández Trujillo, Cándido Ansede, José Marsal, Pedro Menchón, Jaume Calafell, Federico Vélez, and Fonseca; others, such as José Castellanos, Rufino, Pedro Reales, and J. Grimaldos, took up the profession later. Luis Escobar was probably the most typical member of this group of popular photographers. His work in Albacete, during the Civil War, cost him several months in prison and the confiscation of much of his archive of negatives. After this interruption, Escobar went on working as a traveling photographer in the villages of La Manchuela, although the shortage and inferior quality of materials, and a certain bitterness that he never shook off, were the main reasons why his photographs lost much of their freshness, their insight, and the compositional vigor seen in his earlier work.

Antonio Avilés is a similar case; although of lesser ability, he produced some impressive pictures in the first weeks after the war, in Granada province. Menchón, a pupil of José Rodrigo, is also representative of the period. His work is nothing out of the ordinary; he seems simply to have competently pointed his camera at scenes in the streets of his city. His intense

JAIME PACHECO. Gymnastics class in a girls' private school. Vigo, 1940s. (Pacheco Archive)

JUAN ANTONIO AVILÉS. Pupils of the Escuela Nacional de niñas de Doña Augusta González. Orce, Granada, 1941. (Mercedes Avilés Collection)

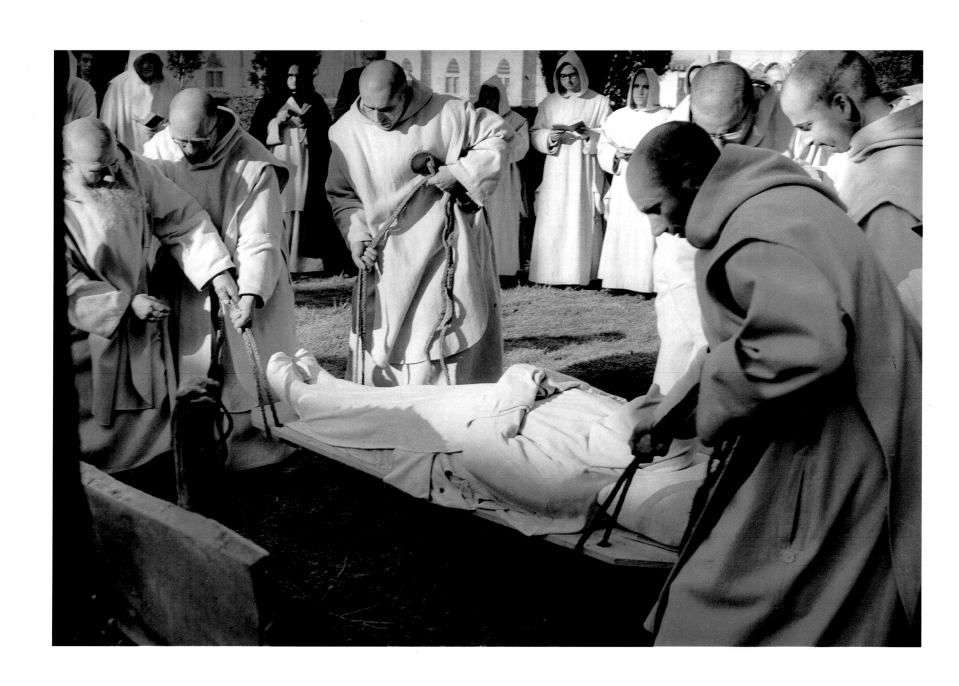

FEDERICO VÉLEZ. Burial at Miraflores Monastery. Burgos, 1967. (Vélez Archive)

JOSÉ CASTELLANOS. Team of harvesters in fields near Villarrobledo, Albacete. 1950s. (Castellanos Archive)

dedication to his profession resulted in some memorable photographs that constitute a comprehensive picture of daily life in Lorca, in those years of patriotic fever.

Manuel Ferrol, of La Coruña, is more unusual. He was a studio portrait photographer and all-purpose photographer who had trained in the photographic associations. As far removed from the technical preciosity of these societies as he was from the theorizing of the so-called "modern" photographers, Ferrol produced a splendid reportage on emigration in 1956, relying exclusively on his insight and talent. Ferrol's language is concise and direct to deliver a message charged with pathos: blurred faces, unconventional and apparently absurd composition, figures half out of the frame, light saturation …. A whole handful of "mistakes" (sometimes simple visual defects on the part of the photographer) and technical faults that not only fail to diminish the documentary value of the reportage but even emphasize its dramatic quality.

Mention should also be made of certain other photographers who, on the fringes of the officialdom of the time, produced valuable work; they include Joaquín Gomis, José Suárez, the Anglo-Spaniard Otho Lloyd, and Francesc Catalá Roca. Gomis, born in 1902, maintained close links with the Catalan artistic circles of his time. His close personal and artistic association with Joan Miró made him the visual chronicler of the latter's life and personal world. He took up photography in about 1920, and after the brief flowering of Spanish photography in the 1930s, developed a taste for the shapes, objects, and details that strongly characterized his limpid, serene, and technically faultless pictures.

Otho Lloyd began his intense dedication to photography in 1940, when he joined the Agrupación Fotográfica de Cataluña. In spite of the enthusiasm for the painterly style that then existed within the society, Lloyd never fell for this approach. Although he worked in a diversity of genres, it was in his pictures of urban locations that his exquisite feeling for composition and light is most clearly appreciated.

José Suárez, known for his excellent series on Galicia, was working on *Mariñeiros*, a documentary movie, when the Civil War broke out. Caught off guard, he was forced into exile in Argentina, where he continued his photographic work. As a press photographer for *La Prensa*, *Life*, and *La Nación*, he spent several months in Japan, where he took a large number of excellent photographs that are full of insight and knowing. After his return to Spain, in 1960 he began an ambitious reportage on the villages of La Mancha, in which his powerful and sure instinct is undiminished, enlivening the barren

JOAQUÍN GOMIS. Joan Miró and Joan Prats examining lithographs as they come off the press at Miralles, the printers. Barcelona, 1944. (Generalitat de Catalunya)

OTHO LLOYD. La Ribera district. Barcelona, 1946. (Salvador Martínez Collection)

MANUEL FERROL. A group of emigrants having their picture taken before leaving for the United States. La Coruña, 1956. (Photographer's collection)

JOSÉ CASTELLANOS. Ploughing in Albacete province. 1950s. (Castellanos Archive)

landscape of Spanish photography with his delicate touch and mastery of observation and composition.

It was Catalá Roca, however, who was the most important photographer of his time and whose work was the most decisively realistic and documentary. His work firmly bridges the gap between avant-garde photography of the prewar period and the new wave of documentary photography of the 1940s and 1950s. He received his technical training from his father, the prestigious photographer Pere Catalá-Pic, inheriting his skill and formal boldness. This can be seen in some of his early work, such as *El pianista* (1936) or his vision of the monument to Christopher Columbus (1951). His photographs, exhibited in 1953 and published in such books as *Tauromaquia* (1953), *Barcelona* (1954), and *Cuenca* (1956), bear the mark of a mature professional who was able at once to combine a sound mastery of technique with a tangible creative flair.

In his work, pure visual instinct and a sure perception of reality seem to predominate over creative freedom and originality. Catalá Roca turned his focused gaze on the essential details of things, with the aim of communicating his own view of the world in a laconic and direct way. "Catalá Roca," wrote Cirici, "is a typical Catalan whose sense of reality is firmly rooted in pragmatism and who bases the value of pictures on the communication of ideas, elevating particular or ephemeral scenes to the status of meaningful archetypes."[11] Firmly rooted in the realms of certainty, Catalá Roca was always very sure of the validity of his own perceptions. This is the characteristic that probably most strongly marks his best photography, and which exerted a decisive influence on the work of the generation of realist photographers that emerged in the 1950s and 1960s.

On another level, only a few short-lived and experimental movements with a small following managed to break the routine imposed by the demands of bourgeois and upper-class society. One such movement was a skirmish led by Gregorio Prieto, Eduardo Chicharro, and Carlos Edmundo de Ory in the 1940s, a trivial, theatrical turn that hardly made any impression on the cultural world of the time. In photographic terms, all that came out of that harmless piece of second-hand surrealism was some low-key and utterly forgettable collage by Gregorio Prieto.

But, besides these innocuous transgressions and the work of those photographers that anticipated documentary realism, Spanish photography of the period could be very adequately summed up by this accurate diagnosis, which Juan Antonio Bardem applied to Spanish cinema in 1955: it was politically ineffectual, socially false, intellectually poor and of very little commercial consequence. This situation was to continue without any change until the years of the transition to democracy.

CATALÁ ROCA. Interval at the Liceo. Barcelona, 1952. (Collection of the heirs of Catalá Roca)

THROUGH FOREIGN EYES

In that context, marked as it was by an academic idealization and technical perfection, images of Spanish life could only be found elsewhere—in the work of some of the great foreign photojournalists, such as Eugene Smith, Henri Cartier-Bresson, Robert Frank, William Klein, Jean Dieuzaide, Inge Morath, and Michael Wolgensinger, who began to come to Spain from 1950; their work espoused a documentary or humanist esthetic that reached its apotheosis in *The Family of Man*, an exhibition organized by Edward Steichen in 1955.[12]

Of these photographers, the one whose work became best known was Eugene Smith, author of the famous *Spanish Village*, which decisively marked the birth of a new concept of photojournalism. Smith was working for *Life* in Paris when he left for Spain on 2 May 1950, accompanied by his assistant Ted Castle and his guide Nina Peinado. It was the first time, since the end of the Spanish Civil War, that the authorities of Franco's regime had allowed a foreign reporter to move about in Spain with a degree of freedom. After they had covered more than 6,500 miles in search of a suitable location, they decided to work in Deleitosa, a village of 2,000 inhabitants in the province of Cáceres. That same month, Smith completed the major part of his photographic essay—the well-known photograph of the Guardia Civil (see page 131) was taken on 22 May. He returned to Madrid on 23 May.

From then on, Smith was fully aware of the importance of this work. "It would be something absolutely irrefutable," he wrote to his mother, "just as were my pictures of the war or my reportage on the country doctor."[13] However, while Castle remained in Madrid developing the film, Smith returned to Deleitosa to take the last of the photographs, although he could not do this since the Guardia Civil were trying to track him down to confiscate the negatives. *The Spanish Village* was finally published in the issue of *Life* dated 9 April 1951. Besides its importance in the mainstream history of photography, Smith's photographic essay constitutes one of the most profound visual testimonies of rural Spain of its time, a moving document of the shape of life and death in a peasant community steeped in centuries-old isolation and—as Smith himself put it— in a fate that demands pride and moral fortitude of a people forced to survive in extremely difficult conditions.

In complete contrast to Smith's vision is that of Jean Dieuzaide, who with Riboud, Boubat, Cartier-Bresson, and Doisneau, was one of the most brilliant exponents of quality French photojournalism. Dieuzaide was sent to Spain in 1951 by the publisher Arthaud, although in 1949 he had already worked there periodically with the

EUGENE SMITH. From *The Spanish Village*. Deleitosa, Cáceres, 1950. (The magazine *Life*)

EUGENE SMITH. From *The Spanish Village*. 1950. (Magnum-Zardoya)

EUGENE SMITH. First communion, from *The Spanish Village.* 1950. (Magnum-Zardoya)

JEAN DIEUZAIDE. Children in front of the Torre del Oro. Seville, 1951. (Dieuzaide Archive)

object of illustrating the book *La España del sur* (Southern Spain). His pictures are imbued with a perception of Spain that is close to the romantic ideal of all that is uncorrupted, uncontaminated, and authentic. Dieuzaide did not seek out the topical or the picturesque, but something that was different. With their extraordinary technical quality, his photographs of Spain are among the most personal, spontaneous, and minutely observed of the period.[14]

Cartier-Bresson's vision is colder and most distant. He arrived in Spain in 1953, to work on his book *The Europeans*, which was published in 1955. Although these photographs do not have the quality of those taken on his early journeys, they bear his personal stamp, his own clarity of vision. Closely related to the vision of Cartier-Bresson is that of Inge Morath, an Austrian photographer who came to Spain in 1953 as Cartier-Bresson's assistant. In April 1954, after experiencing certain difficulties at the frontier, Morath returned to Spain to complete an intensely personal piece of work that went on until 1957. Always avoiding the hackneyed, painterly shot, Morath produced a

comprehensive portrait of Spanish villages and people that breathes sincerity, understanding, and tenderness.[15]

Other notable photographers also worked in Spain, such as the Briton Bert Hardy (1951), the Swede George Oddner (1952), William Klein, Edouard Boubat (1957), and Marc Riboud, who recorded the contrast between real and official Spain with photographs that he took for the controversial *Valley of the Fallen* (1959). In 1952, Robert Frank, a Swiss photographer who was among those who were most strongly to influence contemporary photography, worked in Mallorca, Valencia, and Barcelona.

Other important photographers came to Spain in the 1960s. Among them were Jean Mounicq (1961), Robert Lebeck (1964), Piergiorgio Branzi (1960), Gianni Berengo (1966), Ferdinando Scianna (1969), Lucien Clergue (1965), and Loomis Dean (1960), who illustrated the book *Hemingway's Spain*. When Irving Penn visited Extremadura in 1965, he took an important series of photographs, which were later included in his book *World in a Small Room* (1958). The Swiss photographer Jean Mohr came to Spain for the first time in 1965, and returned there in the early 1970s to work on his well-

WILLIAM KLEIN. Madrid, 1956. (Photographer's collection)

LUCIEN CLERGUE. El Cordobés in the bullring, with red cape. Nîmes, 1965. (Photographer's collection)

M. WOLGENSINGER.
Organ-grinder. Barcelona,
1953. (Wolgensinger Archive)

JEAN MOHR. Emigrant
traveling to Switzerland.
1970. (Mohr Archive)

known reportage on European emigration, published in the book *Le septième homme* (1976, The Seventh Man).

Brassaï, Fulvio Roiter, and Michael Wolgensinger have a different character. All are authors of excellent illustrated guides that were well received by the European postwar public. Brassaï's *Séville en fête* (1954, Fiesta in Seville), although substantially inferior to his more personal photographs of the Parisian artistic fringe, contains some excellent pictures of the city and of the daily life of its inhabitants. Fulvio Roiter worked in 1955 on the illustration of *Andalucía* (1956), a book that contained writings by Unamuno, Lorca, and Juan Ramón Jiménez. More ambitious is the excellent photo-journalism of the Swiss Michael Wolgensinger, author of *Spanien* (1956, Spain), a surprising and exhaustive photographic record that resulted from his numerous journeys in that country in the early 1950s.

The Hungarian Nicolás Muller is an exceptional case. He was forced to leave his country in 1938 to escape Nazism. After short periods in France, Portugal, and Morocco, he finally settled permanently in Madrid in 1947. In that culturally barren landscape, marked by the obsolescence of a tradition of photography that was esthetically bankrupt, Muller's was one of the few minds open to modernity. He was one of a brilliant generation of exiled Hungarian photographers—who also numbered Robert Capa, Brassaï, François Kollar and Martin Munckacsi—and one of the photographers who could best capture reality in postwar Spain. This he did in thousands of photographs published in such books as *España clara* (1966, Spain Revealed) and in some half a dozen illustrated regional guides (1967–68).

Despite the demands of publishers, Muller produced work that is full of dignity, which sidesteps the picturesque subject matter that was so widely exploited by the legions of Spanish photographers who were at pains to show an idealized Spain that existed only in the detached rhetoric of officialdom.

Valca and *Infonal* were two of the dictatorship's favorite national photographic companies. (Miquel Galmes Collection)

ENFORCING THE DICTATORSHIP

The political and economic state of a country in the grip of dictatorship was going to have repercussions on the commercial infrastructure of photography. In the years immediately following the Civil War, it was suffering an even deeper crisis than that which had recurrently dogged it since the end of the golden age of studio portrait photography. Economic conditions, for several years underpinned by the black market, were dire. Photographers were without light-sensitive paper, film, cameras, or even developers, as a result of which many of them had no alternative but to resort to old-fashioned glass negatives or whatever the precarious national movie industry could pass on that was surplus to requirements. In Spain, the attitude had always prevailed that it was other countries that led the way as far as technological innovation was concerned, so the country depended almost entirely on foreign industry. The regime's international isolation made the situation even worse, in that materials could be obtained only from countries that were politically aligned with Spain—notably Germany. These materials reached Spain via official importers who, within limitations imposed by the fixing of import quotas, managed to supply the few specialist photographic manufacturers, such as Eduardo Grünner, Ramón Cortés, Pablo A. Werli, as well as Gaspar Mampel, to whom was subcontracted the manufacture of the best-known foreign models. Authorized import quotas were often exceeded, so that they effectively became a kind of black market in themselves, and this was acknowledged and frequently endorsed by customs officials. Just like medicines and high-priority items, photographic materials attained the status of contraband goods to be traded on the black market.[16]

On another level, the Spanish camera-manufacturing industry had to overcome almost insuperable obstacles. The dictatorship contributed in some measure to the development of a fair number of small-scale national enterprises, whose task it was to adapt their production so as make up the shortfall caused by the absence of imports. Most of them produced cameras designed and patented abroad, even though they faced major problems in trying to obtain suitable optical materials. The first business to manufacture Bakelite cameras was Univex, which flooded the market with its Unica, Supra, Marivex, Winar, Germanic, Olmar, and Argos models. All these were very cheap, basic, and mechanically rudimentary. Between 1942 and 1945, another firm, Industrias Matutano SA, made the popular wooden models called Perfecta and Capta-Baby.

It was not until the 1960s, however, that Cerlex de

Vic in Barcelona came up with something more sophisticated than those elementary cameras, when its famous Werlisa camera went into production. The firm, founded by Pablo Adrián Werli, launched its famous Werlisa Mat, whose plastic design was a stunning commercial success. According to Acereda Valdés, production of these cameras reached 12 million in the 30 years that the factory was in business. [17]

Anaca cameras, too, were highly popular with portrait photographers of the time. Other models of studio camera were manufactured by Garriga, Oliver Salleras, Carceller, and Mampel. The modest national photographic industry even came to produce miniature cameras, even though the increasing economic impetus of Germany and the Asian countries eventually put paid to those romantic achievements of the dictatorship. Meanwhile, production of such materials as light-sensitive paper and film was practically monopolized by two firms, Valca and Negra, although small concerns such as Infonal, Mafe (Manufacturas Fotográficas Españolas), and Supremus also played their part. Valca (Sociedad Española de Productos Fotográficos Valca) began by manufacturing plates for Artes Gráficas, and went on to produce photographic paper, film, and chemical products. The establishment of Valca was a real beacon of hope, and it was enthusiastically welcomed by the specialist press. As Enrique Goizueta wrote in the July 1944 issue of the magazine *Sombras*, "The firm that in Spain undertook with unshakeable drive and confidence the great and difficult task of manufacturing the complete range of photographic materials would of necessity be capable of downsizing so as to form a single entity in the line-up of firms that are predestined not by virtue of their size or lineage, since this firm is neither large nor in possession of distinguished ancestry, but through bold audacity and noble presumption to bestow upon themselves the titles 'new' and 'the first in Spain' … Domestic production is now under way. Let us be glad of it and let us wish it many years prosperity and success, as a demonstration of the fact that in Spain confidence and potential are rock solid."

In 1939, Negra i Tort, for its part, resumed the manufacture of paper, which it had begun in 1916. The Civil War had forcibly interrupted production and in the early 1940s the firm experienced serious difficulty in obtaining suitable raw materials. Up until 1959, with the easing of import restrictions, Negra's factories supplied the bulk of the 95 percent of photographic materials used in Spain. In 1952, the firm offered a wide range of papers—the popular Negtor papers—making it one of the most competitive companies in Europe in its field.

Alongside these major players in the Spanish photographic industry in the postwar years were other, smaller concerns, such as Mafe, which manufactured products patented by Perutz and which eventually became part of Agfa, and Infonal (Industria Fotoquímica Nacional), founded in 1928 by Rafael Garriga, which in 1942 was producing some of the highest-quality film available. According to Acereda Valdés, Garriga manufactured cameras and papers for minute hands and was the author of one of the few Spanish theoretical texts of his time.

The absence of a real national industry capable of supplying the needs of professional photographers in Spain was occasionally mitigated by sheer ingenuity. One has only to think of the famous electronic flash, named Daf, invented in 1951 by Francesc Alguersuari, and which was used in place of the old magnesium flashes. Many professional photographers used this flash until the introduction of a wide range of other more sophisticated imports, such as the well-known Vacublitz.

The precarious Spanish photographic industry, into which German, American, and Japanese products were daily making inroads, never achieved sufficient growth nor managed to satisfy the needs of domestic consumers. In 1980—more than 40 years after the end of the Civil War—annual production hardly reached 6,000 million pesetas. That year there were three firms specializing in the manufacture of photographic materials: Mafe, with an annual turnover of 2,273 million pesetas and funded with 40 percent German capital; Negra Industrial, funded by Spanish capital totalling 2,061 million pesetas; and Valca, funded by English capital and having an annual turnover of 1,796 million pesetas. Between them these three firms employed a workforce of 1,300 people, and their joint annual investment reached 4,000 million pesetas. Exports were negligible, barely reaching 1,490 million pesetas a year, while in 1979 imports totalled no less than 6,510 million pesetas.[18]

Neither did legislation aid the situation, since the Stabilization Plan of 1959 meant the end of state subsidies for Spanish businesses. Taxation laws that came into effect in 1974 treated photography like a luxury that was "inessential and superfluous," as a result of which this sector was severely damaged. On the eve of the measure coming into effect, the manufacturers themselves did not neglect to express the unease they felt toward what they saw as an attempt to destroy the national photographic industry. "In no way," proclaimed the bulletin *Ecos Negra* in 1968, "can photography be considered a luxury … Spanish production of light-sensitive papers serves an industrial, professional, cultural, and commercial market that absorbs a very high percentage of its output, and materials commonly referred to as those used by amateurs account for not 5 percent of the total volume of this output. Labeling photographic materials as luxury items will not materially assist the current aims of taxation… The only result of this policy will be the closure of factories in Spain."[19] Fiscal policy itself and increasing foreign competition eventually broke the feeble resolve of the Spanish photographic industry, culminating in the closure of such leading concerns as Negra and Valca, in the early 1990s.

On the other hand, consumer demand was not very encouraging either. According to figures published in the magazine *Foto Profesional*, the average number of photographs taken by every Spaniard was eight per year in 1986. This equalled 0.4 rolls of film per person per year, as opposed to 2.8 in the United States, 2.2 in Switzerland, 1.9 in Japan, 1.4 in France, and 1.1 in the United Kingdom. After 40 years of official neglect, ignorance, and rigid legal and trade union control, photography in Spain was in a parlous state. "The field of professional photography," stated José Aumente, president of the Agrupación Nacional de Fotógrafos Profesionales in 1972, "is compromised not only by unfair competition from a

Advertisement for the *Captaflex* camera. 1953. (Gerardo Acereda Collection)

large number of interlopers but also from a large number of professionals, all firmly rooted in the industrial small-holding one associates with an underdeveloped profession. The general attitude of professional photographers in Spain is one that is conformist and absurd."[20]

The situation became so serious that, in no small number of meetings and conferences, businessmen in this sector went so far as to request the establishment of specialist schools of photography and to propose that photography become part of the national curriculum. However, it was obvious that, for the State, photography was of interest only from a fiscal point of view. Treasury Department tax-collecting zeal led to the establishment of the so-called Carnet de Empresa con Responsabilidad, under the direct control of the administration of the trade unions. This identity card was vital for any kind of professional activity, and the teaching of photography was regulated by a law passed by the Department of Education and Science on 11 February 1966.

Nevertheless, despite these official recommendations, Spanish photographers continued to be virtually self-taught. "How does one learn photography in Spain?" wondered Manuel López Rodríguez in 1985. "Where does one train as a press photographer, an industrial

photographer, a fashion photographer, or an advertising photographer? At schools of photography? Is there a university that teaches the mechanics of photography? The answer, up until now, is none other than ministerial silence; it is the only possible response for the simple reason that, as far as a specialist training is concerned, nothing is available beyond the schools of applied arts, which have recently closed down, thus barring one very modest avenue to vocational training."[21]

Even in 1986, despite the fact that 16,000 photographic laboratories had been installed in German schools, the teaching of photography in Spain was not an issue with the EGB (Educación General Básica), nor was it considered by the Facultad de Ciencias de la Información itself. This marginalization was denounced during the *Primeras Jornadas Catalanas de Fotografía*, which took place in Barcelona in 1980, and the educational bodies responsible were accused of relegating photography to the academic ghetto of private establishments.

Among the latter must be singled out the Institut d'Estudis Fotogràfics de Catalunya (1972), which, at the instigation of Miquel Galmes, paid special attention to the teaching of photography, as well as to the rehabilitation of forgotten photographers and the preservation of photographic archives. Four years later, the Centros de Enseñanza de la Imagen (CEI) were established in Madrid and Barcelona.

As far as the market for photography was concerned, the outlook was no more encouraging. According to Valeriano Bozal, the Spanish art market was suffering every kind of precapitalist practice, being more firmly based on barter between a small number of initiates than on the system of buying and selling that is characteristic of industrially developed, liberal societies. Only from the 1960s could the stirrings of activity in this field be discerned, with the opening of one or two galleries that were to play a decisive part in the marketing of works of art. Photography, however, which culturally was not held in high esteem, which was underdeveloped from an industrial point of view, continued to be treated as no more than a servant of the arts or as a subordinate activity with no real relevance.

Consequently, neither the economic lift-off heralded by the technocrats nor the effects of the self-proclaimed Spanish economic miracle could lead to the creation of the slightest commercial infrastructure in this field. That did not occur until 1970, when Tino Calabuig opened Spain's first photographic gallery, in Madrid. His example was followed in other cities such as Barcelona, Zaragoza, Valencia, and Tarragona, but without encouraging results. In 1980 there were around ten photographic galleries in Spain, and a number of very insignificant businesses. Funded quite generously by a small number of international manufacturers such as Canon, these galleries made a commendable effort to promote photography not only on a commercial level but also in an educational sense. Most of them, besides fulfilling the role of exhibition halls and salerooms, also became ad hoc libraries, schools, and specialist warehouses.

After a few years of uneventful existence, the majority of these galleries closed down one by one as photography gradually came to be exhibited in state-run museums and galleries, and as an incipient publishing program began, led by Blume, Gustavo Gili, and most notably Lunwerg. "I believe that the photographic galleries have completed their mission," said Joan Fontcuberta in 1985. "Photographers of Miserachs' and Maspons' generation fought for the recognition that their profession rightly deserved, and they got it. The next generation demands to be granted the status of artists, of creators." "Photography that is 'useless', that has no patrons, that has no ostensible purpose," wrote Xavier Miserachs nine years later, "has, from its very beginning, had to be marketed through art dealers and galleries, in the expectation of a thriving culture of public or private collecting that never seems to materialize. It must be said

Spanish-made cameras were widely used by amateur photographers during the postwar years. (Gerardo Acereda Collection)

that it is this economic mechanism, and the speculation that it generates, that has been one of the factors responsible for bringing painting to its present standstill. To the 'creative' photographer, however, the theme seems irrelevant, in the hope that the way is not in the photography market but in the art market."[22]

That old pictorialist aspiration—to raise photography to the ranks of the fine arts—was now espoused by younger generations of photographers, provoking certain excesses designed to fuel the hope among art dealers of creating a market for photographs bathed in the aura of the unique work of art. This, a new departure, was a question of taming photography, forcing it to submit to esthetic canons previously sanctioned by the conventional art market; as a result, the framework of creative latitude as an autonomous language was dangerously curtailed. In response to this development, critics quickly sounded the alarm. "Among contemporary photographers," wrote José María Artero in 1976, "there is a tendency to sign a limited number of prints, then destroy the original negative. Thus the photograph in its own right becomes part of a market that values anything that is rare or unique."[23]

While there was an almost total lack of any kind of framework for exhibiting, marketing, distributing, or publishing their work, Spanish photographers—amateurs and a large number of professionals—had recourse only to societies, associations, groups, and competitions, and the few magazines that came out in those deprived years.

RANIERO FERNÁNDEZ.
Antilles. 1950s.
(Photographer's collection,
Centro de Estudios
Fotográficos de Vigo)

SOCIETIES AND ASSOCIATIONS

The Civil War had condemned photography in Spain to profound bankruptcy, and also those institutions that had up until then been its cornerstones—for example, the Real Sociedad Fotográfica de Madrid, the Agrupacíon Fotográfica de Cataluña, the Photo-Club of Valencia, and the Sociedad Fotográfica de Zaragoza. The work carried out by these historical establishments was extremely limited in the early 1940s, following the reorganization of their boards of directors and the resumption of work by their mainly middle-class members, the winners in the crusade against communism. The Agrupación Fotográfica de Cataluña, whose president was Manuel Vallespí Serra, was the most active of the institutions, organizing a major program of exhibitions.

The Real Sociedad Fotográfica de Madrid, meanwhile, resumed its activities in 1940, under the presidency of Count de la Ventosa and with José Tinoco, Eduardo Susanna, Francisco Andrada, Sebastián Castedo, and Diego Gálvez on its board of directors. In Valencia, the Photo-Club maintained an intermittent existence until 1947, when Vicente Peydró was still its president. As to the Sociedad Fotográfica de Zaragoza, which had been able to continue holding its international exhibitions during the Civil War through the support of the Sociedad Fotográfica Italiana, maintained a modest program of exhibitions thanks to the work of Aurelio Grasa, Pascual Nogueras, Lorenzo Almarza, Jalón Ángel, Gil Marraco,

Pascual Martín Triep, and Manuel Serrano.

Beyond this, it was difficult to launch new societies on account of the dictatorship's administrative obstacles. In their articles of association, societies were required to state clearly that their existence was strictly concerned with photography, and to guarantee that they would not nurture in their ranks works of a "realist or immoral" character that might inconvenience the all-powerful civil government. "It was very hard to obtain permission to form a society," remembers Federico Bermúdez, the driving force behind the formation of the Agrupación Fotográfica Gallega. "We had to elect as president José Bellver, president of the supreme court, and admit senior police figures as members."[24]

As a result, few societies or associations were established during those years. One of the most prominent was the Agrupación Fotográfica Gallega, which was founded in 1946 by such amateur photographers as Luis Zamora, Raniero Fernández, Manuel García Ferrer, Francisco Losada, Veiga Roel, and Inocencio Smith de las Heras. The Agrupación Fotográfica Valenciana was established in 1947, under the auspices of the Obra Sindical de Educación y Descanso, and run by José Furió, José Asensi, and Manuel Hernández. That same year saw the formation of the Agrupación Fotográfica de Guipúzcoa in San Sebastian by a small nucleus of amateur photographers headed by the Marquess of Rocaverde. Among the members of the Agrupación Fotográfica de Guipúzcoa, Bernardo de Aurrecoechea, Alberto Fernández Ibarburu, and Juan Ángel Arrieta deserve special mention. In 1945 they had formed the Peña Fotográfica de Elche and the Peña Hidroquinona, which would become the Sociedad Fotográfica de Sevilla.

These administrative strictures eased with time, until the feeble economic upturn brought about the democratization of the art of photography that, in the 1940s, had been within reach of the middle classes alone. Of equal importance was the work carried out by the Obra Sindical de Educación y Descanso, an organization that supported the political regime, and under whose auspices dozens of associations were established. These eventually metamorphosed into a "great family" of amateur photographers at the center of which there developed what J. D. Bisbal described as "comradeship and friendship between fellow photographers." These associations revived the "photographic outings" of earlier years, organized short courses and lessons in laboratory work, and maintained premises in discreet locations that allowed their members to exchange ideas.

The heyday of the photographic societies came in the 1950s. The Agrupación Fotográfica Almeriense, formed in 1950, was followed in 1952 by the Peña del Café

Español de La Coruña, which spawned the Sociedad Fotográfica de La Coruña (SOFOCO), which formed part of the Obra Sindical de Educación y Descanso. In 1955 the Agrupación Fotográfica y Cinematográfica de Navarra was founded in Pamplona and run by Manuel María Castell, Pedro María Irurzun, Nicolás Ardanaz, Fernando Galle, Félix Elbusto, and José María Bayona. In 1956, again under the auspices of the Obra Sindical de Educación y Descanso, were founded the Agrupación Fotográfica de Guadalajara, headed by Santiago Bernal and Félix Ortego, and Alto Duero, a society whose president was Manuel Lafuente Caloto.

Despite their pompous titles and pretentious meetings, these were modest, intimate associations, most occupying very small, rented premises.[25] Nevertheless, they were the only bodies to keep alight the flame of interest in photography through times of severe constraint. Their humble premises became makeshift schools, where those whose interest in photography had been forcibly neglected in the postwar years could learn the basics of photographic technique, meet others, and share ideas. Their short courses, conferences, and exhibitions constituted their meager theoretical base, at a time when specialist establishments did not exist. Neither, because of the political regime's isolation, did the faintest echo of the international photographic scene reach the country. "The Sociedad Fotográfica de Reus," recalled Josep María Ribas Prous, "was hardly active at all during the 1960s. We, its members, would meet in a kind of lumber room lent by the town hall, where we would discuss photography and yearn for foreign magazines. Some of those who had traveled told us that outside Spain you could buy all manner of books and magazines that were prohibited here. From the viewpoint of our modest association, Spain seemed to us like a concentration camp, while culture in all its forms was something that existed on the other side of the border."

The very inertia that beset their operations, the stultification brought about by routine, and the immovable attitude of their directors soon dulled the spirit of these associations. They eventually became mere social clubs or leisure centers, even though in 1972 an official directive obliged them to call themselves "Entidades Artísticas Colaboradoras." This decree was barely effective, on the one hand because of the gravity of the problem that it aimed to solve and on the other because of the precarious political position of a regime living out its final days. The crisis faced by these societies became uncontainable, despite attempts to breathe new life into them in the 1950s and 1960s by such outstanding figures as Luis Conde Vélez, Gerardo Vielba, Gabriel Cualladó, and Ribas Prous, and of such key members of the younger generation as José Antonio Duce and Rafael Navarro in Zaragoza; Pio Guerendiaín, Koldo Chamorro, and Carlos Cánovas in Pamplona; Gonzalo Vinagre and Ton Sirera in Lérida; Salvador Obiols in Barcelona; Manuel Cruzado Cazador in Castellón; Saturnino Espín in Murcia; and Jorge Rueda, Elías Dolcet, Antonio Tabernero, and Rafael

Levenfeld in Madrid. The creation of centers of learning and official courses, and the launch of new magazines and specialist periodicals, plunged the associations into even deeper crisis, even though in the 1980s new societies were formed in Castilla-León, Andalucía, and Extremadura. Among them was the Agrupación Fotográfica de Córdoba (AFOCO), established in 1981 and headed by José Gálvez, Alicia Reguera, and Juan Vacas. At the present time, these associations are languishing, victims of their own inward-looking attitude and the fact that they offer little to their members. Nevertheless, some of them have revamped themselves, looking back to their origins. Such institutions as the RSF in Madrid, AFOCO in Córdoba, and AFZ in Zaragoza have recently begun a program of cataloging, restoring and exhibiting their collections; outstanding in this field is the pioneering work begun in 1975 by J. M. Ribas Prous at the Agrupación Fotográfica de Reus.

For more than half a century, the existence of these associations generated an esthetic that found expression in the world of exhibitions and whose morbid influence weighed down the work of several generations of photographers. That hierarchy of merit was creating an aristocracy of photographers, which consisted of the most typical practitioners of high-flown academism and technical perfection that was the trademark of the associations themselves. However, these societies did produce photographers whose work was conspicuously interesting, although it was inevitably indebted to neopictorialism's saccharine esthetic. Within the AFG, noteworthy in this respect are Luis Zamora, Raniero Fernández, Luis Rueda, Manuel García Ferrer, and José Veiga Roel.

In the Photo-Club of Valencia, outstanding work was produced by members of El Forat, a group founded in 1962 by José Segura Gavilá, Francisco Sanchís, Francisco Soler Montalar, and José Miguel de Miguel. José García Ferrada, a member of the Agrupación San Juan Bosco de Burriana since 1962, produced work that captured the simplicity of daily life. Most interesting is the work of Cruzado Cazador, a member of the Agrupación Fotográfica de Castellón, who pioneered the anthropological approach in photography. The work of Pedro María Irur-

JUAN VACAS. *Cotton pickers collect their wages.* 1970. (Photographer's collection)

JORDI OLIVÉ. *Big brother's shadow.* 1960. (Agrupación Fotográfica de Reus)

LEONARDO CANTERO.
El herradero. 1959. (Centro
Nacional de Arte Reina Sofía)

zun, Nicolás Ardanaz, and Félix Aliaga (a classic competition photographer), all members of the AFN, also deserves mention, as do the following: in Andalucía, that of Emigdio Mariani and of Juan Vacas, of Córdoba; among associates of the Agrupación Fotográfica del Casino de Comercio de Tarrasa, that of Jordi Vilaseca Parramón and other members of the El Mussol group such as José María Albero, A. Moncaujussá, and Ignacio Marroyo; among members of the RSF de Madrid, that of Leonardo Cantero, Rafael Romero, Gregorio Merino, Sigfrido de Guzmán, Juan Antonio Sáenz, and Nieto Canedo; among members of the AFC, that of Jaume Jorba Aulés, Ramón Vilalta Sensada, Pedro Martínez Carrión, an excellent press photographer, and Pere Sender, whose painterly work evolved to a documentary style full of charm and spontaneity.

In the AFC, Carmelo Tartón Vinuesa, Martín Triep, and José Antonio Duce were particularly revelant. In Castile, mention should be made of Santiago Bernal, president of the Agrupación Fotográfica de Guadalajara, and José Núñez Larraz, who left the Agrupación Fotográfica de Salamanca to join the Grupo Libre de Fotografía, which, moving away from figurative photography, tended toward abstraction. In this respect his work is related to that of Ángel Quintas, of Zamora, who produced some significant work. Two others, whose work approached abstraction, are Ángel Úbeda, of La Mancha, and Ton Sirera, of Lérida; both died young.

Prominent members of the Agrupación Fotográfica de Reus were Josep Massó, Salvador Ferré, and Josep María

Ribas Prous, pioneer of nude photography and a notable press photographer. Jordi Olivé, founder of the Agrupación Fotográfica de La Alforja, is also of note. With no trace of artistic confection, he knew how to penetrate the reality of ordinary people's lives, with his simple, thoughtful, and moving images. A meticulous and precise technique gives Olivé the humility and intuition of the great masters of popular photography, and has resulted in one of the most accurate and penetrating portraits of a small Spanish rural community.

The photographic associations were the prime movers behind the creation of specialist magazines. Many of these were established from within the associations themselves: this was the case of *Sombras* and *Afal*; others, like *Arte Fotográfico*, were the associations' official publications. *Sombras* was launched in June 1944 as the official publication of the Real Sociedad Fotográfica. Founded by Domingo de Luis, the magazine was a platform for neopictorialism, the ethic cultivated by its most assiduous contributors, among whom were Ortiz Echagüe, José Tinoco, Francisco Andrada, Count Ventosa, Eduardo Susanna, Plá Janini, Mora Carbonell, Vicente Peydró, and the Marquess of Santa María del Villar. For over six years, the magazine published only the work of these photographers, together with that of some of their younger followers. Thus the pages of *Sombras* were filled with countless pictures of shepherds, horsemen, castles, Moorish palaces, altar boys, monks, mystics, and friars. Under the editorship of Eduardo

CARMELO TARTÓN.
Prying Eyes. c. 1960.
(Photographer's collection)

J. A. SÁENZ LÓPEZ. *Little boy with a bicycle.* 1965.
(Sáenz López Collection)

GREGORIO MERINO. *In the Lucero district.* Madrid, 1960.
(Photographer's collection)

Vellilla, *Sombras* ceased to be the organ of the Real Socie-dad Fotográfica, and began a new life in which Julio Anoro, Juan María Ardizone (heir of the historic company Kaulak), Pedro María Irurzun, José A. Lassala and, most particularly, Juan Domingo Bisbal, Miguel Tubáu, and Ignacio Barceló played a conspicuous role. After suffering from a lack of direction during the editorship of Ventura and Batalla Altamirano, *Sombras* survived only until 1952. It had failed in its aim to become the mouthpiece of the photographic associations, an objective that was finally achieved by Ignacio Barceló, who, in January 1952, launched the influential magazine *Arte Fotográfico.*

From its beginnings, *Arte Fotográfico* bore the stamp of the official mouthpiece of the photographic associations, whose members, bereft of specialist publications, had felt the lack of a central forum. Editorially, *Arte Fotográfico*'s great merit was precisely its ability to stimulate the associations to contribute enthusiastically, making it the heavyweight magazine "of national relevance and published to serve the needs

of photography" that J. Domingo Bisbal had petitioned for in the pages of the humble newsletter of the Agrupación Fotográfica de Igualada. The editorial philosophy of the magazine was to act as the official forum of the photo-graphic associations, acting as mirror and spokesman for their activities and for the national photographic industry's interests. In its heyday, the print-run reached a creditable 25,000 copies per issue.

As an offshoot of *Sombras, Arte Fotográfico* inherited its spirit and its contributors, which consisted of such prominent neopictorialists as Susanna, Andrada, Tinoco, the Marquess of Santa María del Villar, and the in-evitable Ortiz Echagüe, as well as a sizeable corpus of the movement's younger adherents, among whom were José Loygorry, Diego Gálvez, J. Domingo Bisbal, José María Marca, José de la Higuera, Arcilaga, and Ignacio Barceló himself, who, since taking up the editorship, had become the spiritual leader of the world of asso-ciations and exhibitions. For him, the magazine's most important regular features were official announcements

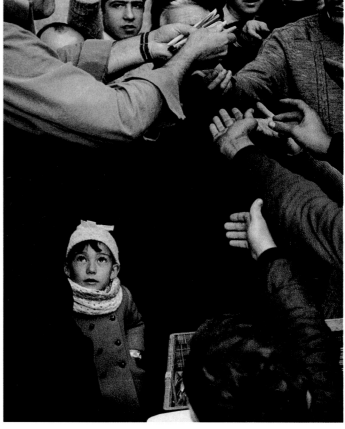

PERE SENDER. The local movie theater. Barcelona, c. 1955. (Private collection)

MARTÍNEZ CARRIÓN. Street vendor. Barcelona, 1960. (Photographer's collection)

and competition results, along with the publication of the prize-winning works and the society page that chronicled the activities of the associations. For more than 30 years, the pages of *Arte Fotográfico* were the inevitable pulpit from which illustrious mediocrity exerted a decisive influence, being held up to naïve provincial photographers as the desideratum of art photography. In this sense, *Arte Fotográfico* was a decidedly obsolete magazine, resistant to change, fossilized and reactionary. But, like the associations themselves, it was also a useful source of specialist information for all those involved in photography at the time but who found themselves without a forum for the exchange of ideas, or for the promotion and exhibition of their work. Through contributions by Roger Doloy, Daniel Masclet, and Emmanuel Sougez, the magazine was also instrumental in making known the work of relevant foreign photographers.

The *Revista Bimestral de Fotografía y Cine*, published by the Asociación Fotográfica Almeriense (Afal), was launched in January 1956 by José María Artero and Carlos Pérez Siquier, who soon after set up an editorial board that included Oriol Maspons, Xavier Miserachs, Gonzalo Juanes, Ricard Terré, and Gabriel Cualladó.

Published in Almería, one of the Spanish provinces most stricken by poverty and emigration, the newsletter was completely unsubsidized, so that its appearance was erratic and its existence beset by problems. Despite its modesty, *Afal* soon became spokesman for and mirror of the new documentary realism of the 1950s and 1960s. Casademont went so far as to describe this movement as the second Spanish photographic avant-garde. It was an avant-garde that, like the one that emerged during the Republican years, departed radically from the pugnacious criticism of the reigning pictorialism.

The pages of *Afal* featured the work of the leading exponents of documentary realism of the 1950s and 1960s: among them were Ramón Masats, Leopoldo Pomés, Joan Colom, Paco Ontañón, Alberto Schommer, Ricard Terré, Gonzalo Juanes, Gabriel Cualladó, Julio Ubiña, Oriol Maspons, Paco Gómez, Cubaró, Jordi Vilaseca, and Pérez Siquier himself. But the magazine was not solely a platform for new-wave Spanish photography; it also tracked new international currents, by using such contributors as Gonzalo Juanes (who showed the work of Irving Penn, William Klein, Robert Frank, and Richard Avedon), Roger Doloy, A. Thevenez and J. A. Chnoll, and publishing translations of articles that had appeared in such periodicals as *Camera*, *Jeune Photography*, *Photorama*, *U.S. Camera*, and *Vita Fotografica*. *Afal* also organized exhibitions in Spain of the work of Edward Weston, Henri Cartier-Bresson, the 30x40 group from Paris, Jeune Photographie Belge, Edward Steichen, and Otto Steinert, to whom the magazine dedicated a special issue in 1961, ten years after he had shown his subjective work, which was to have such an influence on art photography of the period.[26] Circulation of *Afal* settled down to around 2,000 copies per issue; of these only 150 accounted for the membership in Almería, the rest being distributed in photographic circles in Spain and abroad. From 1958, the year that it issued its first and excellent yearbook, the newsletter managed to survive various crises to become a major presence until 1963, when shortage of funds forced it to close.

The baton was taken up by *Imagen y Sonido*. Launched in 1963 under the editorship of Josep María Casademont, the magazine became the platform for a tame style of documentary photography in the shadow of the new realist orthodoxy. *Imagen y Sonido* always maintained close links with the world of the photographic societies, although it countered their wizened academism with a certain reforming zeal.

Besides announcements and competition results, portfolios of winning works, and an occasional article on a historiographic subject by Lluch Oliveres, the magazine occasionally carried articles by Roger Doloy or Xavier Miserachs, or the work of such photographers as Mario Giacomelli, Gianni Berengo, Jean Dieuzaide, Jean Cousin, and Jacques Molniere. The Spanish photographers whose work appeared most often were J. M. Hervás, Paco Ontañón, Juan Dolcet, Jorba Aulés, Ramón Vilalta Sensada, Pedro Martínez Carrión, Eugenio Forcano, Francisco Jarque, Julio Ubiña, Xavier Miserachs, Oriol Maspons, Alberto Hernando Jorbá, Joan Colom, and José María Albero.

In 1969 Casademont was replaced as editor by G. Pasias Lomelino, although he maintained links with the magazine by contributing articles under the by-line Aquiles Pujol. In 1969, doubtless at his instigation, *Imagen y Sonido* began publishing collections of work by the brothers Jaume and Jordi Blassi, while Gabriel Querol became its photographic critic and reporter. In this new phase, alongside the work of the Blassi brothers, the magazine began to publish work by a few members of the younger generation, such as Colita, Toni Catany, Morgan and Gonzalo Vinagre. *Imagen y Sonido* made a bid for an extended lease of life through *Eikonos* which, launched in 1975 under the editorship of Casademont himself, had an ephemeral existence.

In 1972, after obvious years of delay, there appeared

on the scene *Cuadernos de Fotografía*, whose founder and editor was Fernando Gordillo, and whose editorial directors consisted of Cualladó, Paco Gómez, Leonardo Cantero, Vielba, Fernando de Giles, and Pedro Pascual. Produced to a very high standard, the magazine published exclusively the work of photographers who were close to the editorial group, with the exceptional inclusion of one outsider, and regular contributions from certain prominent members of the world of letters and journalism of the period, such as Castro Villacañas, Juan Van Halen, Manuel Alcántara, and Antonio Gibello. *Cuadernos de Fotografía* was published very much as a cross-current—*Nueva Lente* had appeared just one year previously—and, in the eleven issues of its existence, it took a markedly conservative stance, as a result attracting much criticism from younger, more radical sectors.[27]

Apart from these magazines (we shall return to *Nueva Lente* later), in the postwar years there was little more available to those concerned with photography, discounting the modest bulletins of the photographic associations. Of this latter genre perhaps the most interesting was the bulletin published by the Agrupación Fotográfica de Cataluña: it consisted of some 20 pages presented in a straightforward manner and containing information about the social functions and competitions run by the association. Occasionally, there were book reviews and articles signed by such old hands as Lluch Oliveres, who ran a "women's photography section" compiled by Gloria Salas de Villavechia, Carmen García de Ferrando,

J. M. RIBAS PROUS. *In the wind.* 1969. (Agrupación Fotográfica de Reus. Obra Cultural Caixa de Tarragona.)

Sombras, April 1945 issue. (Photograph by A. CAMPAÑÁ)

The magazine *Afal*, March–April 1957 issue. (Photograph by R. TERRÉ)

J. JORBA AULES. *The gang*, winner of the Premio Egara, 1964. (Photographer's collection)

MIGUEL DE MIGUEL. *Showing off*. 1968. (Galería Visor Collection)

and Rosario Martínez Rochina. The bulletin issued by the Real Sociedad Fotográfica de Madrid was an even more modest affair, although in 1960 it was much improved by contributions from Gabriel Cualladó, Gerardo Vielba, Nieto Canedo, Ignacio Barceló, and Paco Ontañón. In 1969 Jorge Rueda, Elías Dolcet, Miguel Oriola, and Cristina García Rodero and others among the more enterprising members of the younger generation became contributors.

Competitions were another mainstay of conservative academic photography in Spain in the postwar years. The origins of such competitions lay in the photographic associations, but they were not restricted to that circuit and soon began to enjoy the sponsorship of town and regional councils, banks, and other commercial establishments. In the barren cultural landscape of the time, competitions gave photographers a unique opportunity to gain recognition by showing their work. Besides, in the words of Ignacio Barceló, they were the only means of winning popularity and functioned as a "school of technical, moral, and personal" training. At a time when decorative photography was all the rage, the quality of the work that was submitted for these competitions was judged in terms of how it measured up to the notions of judges who set great store by the pictorialist and technical esthetic that was upheld by the associations themselves.

The inevitable result was sentimental, undistinguished, and formulaic work. "Ten, fifteen, or even twenty years without a market," wrote Miserachs in 1965,

"have made the basest amateurs out of people who, interested in photography as a source of personal esthetic satisfaction, regarded competitions as the only showcase for their experiments and the only reward for their skills. This led to a proliferation of a style of photography that aspired to be nothing more than fit for competitions, that was profoundly pictorialist, and that rapidly acquired a set of rules and values that were consistent with what was needed to maximize the chance of winning."[28]

Running counter to the didactic esthetic of these competitions and exhibitions, a certain rebellion was brewing. Its paradigm was to be found in the lucid and radical insight of Oriol Maspons, who in 1957 coined the term *salonismo* (exhibitionism) to define the endemic preoccupation with competitions that characterized the era. By *salonismo* Maspons meant that phenomenon that institutionalized a type of photography "that goes on being pictorial," whose only objective was to win prizes, and that thus submits to the demands of judges steeped in the directives of the associations and who stand as the zealous guardians of the most fossilized orthodoxy. "Salon photography," he wrote, "is rather like an old 'player piano'. If, as sometimes happens, it is technical accomplishment, however superficial, that gives it its value, this is because of the vacuity of the subject matter ... 'Art' photography becomes pretentious and is ultimately ridiculous. The word 'art,' by dint of being gratuitously applied, has lost is meaning as far as photography is

concerned. It is better to set it aside for a while, seeing that its meaning has been so devalued."[29]

In the 1950s, the associations made moves to overhaul photographic competitions, alarmed at the increasing disrepute into which they had fallen. A major reform was made by Luis Conde Vélez (pseudonym of Luis Navarro), who in 1954 organized the first national competition for a new type of photography, conceived as a "quest for reality—a personal and subjective interpretation." The contest, which was to be titled the Salón de Fotografía de Vanguardia, was finally sponsored by the Agrupación Fotográfica de Cataluña, after the death of its promoter.

Other developments included the establishment of the Trofeo Egara, organized by the Agrupación Fotográfica del Casino de Comercio de Tarrasa in 1955, and five years later the institution of the Salón de Fotografía Actual by the Real Sociedad Fotográfica de Madrid. This timid emergence of the salon exhibition even had an effect on the Premio Negtor, instituted in 1953 by Higinio Negra and in photographic circles regarded as the top

competition.[30] From 1970, this major commercial contest attracted a sizeable corpus of submissions from the most forward-looking sectors.

In 1974 the prize was awarded to J. M. Oriola for a photomontage; other prize-winners included photographers whose work placed them firmly in the avant-garde: Elías Dolcet, Saturnino Espín, Joan Fontcuberta, José A. Marín Chacón, Salvador Obiols, and Gonzalo Vinagre. The previous year, the Trofeo Egara was won by Morgan, a photographer exploring conceptualism and abstraction. However, this renewal could not materialize, for Spanish photography was too hidebound to break the old salon framework. The absence of any means of promotion, marketing, and publishing continued to act as a constraint on Spanish photography. As a result of this harsh reality, the medium of the competition was, and remains, the only opportunity for photographers to show and promote their work; it was also, as Campañá put it in 1961, "the necessary spur for developing photography's artistic potential."

PÍO GUERENDIAIN. *Challenge*, winner of the Premio Negtor, 1973. (Photographer's collection)

J. M. ORIOLA. Photomontage awarded the Premio Negtor in 1975. (Ecos Negra)

SALVADOR OBIOLS. *Homage to Javier Verdejo*, winner of the Premio Nacional de Fotografía de Autor, 1976. (Obiols Archive)

JOSÉ LOYGORRY. Traveling portrait photographer. 1950s. (Vielba Family Collection)

THE LAST PORTRAIT PHOTOGRAPHERS

Professional photography in Spain in 1939 can be summed up quite simply as portrait photography. The cultural anemia brought about by the dictatorship reduced professional photographers to the most agonizing straits. As the Salamancan photographer Cándido Ansede pointed out in 1949, "What we as provincial photographers do most is portrait photography, the aspect of our work that the general public most appreciates."

Those were no times to be showing off one's artistic capabilities; through long years of shortage, fear, and deprivation, what customers demanded were regular portraits. That year, 90 percent of Spanish photographers were portrait photographers, and that precarious trade was the mainstay of professional photographers, who had survived the disasters of war and the postwar years; these circumstances condemned some of those who had been the most prestigious press photographers of the prewar period to make their living by working as itinerant photographers, traveling to small towns and villages. A classic case is that of Alfonso Sánchez Portela; like many of his generation, he found himself reduced to joining the numberless legion of portrait photographers who traveled the length and breadth of the country during what were popularly referred to as "the hungry years."

Work as traveling photographers once again became the most common recourse among provincial portrait photographers. Like earlier generations, the itinerants of the postwar years put together makeshift sets in patios and farmyards, in school classrooms, or even in the street. The props were whatever objects came to hand: odd things were fetched out of the nearest houses or brought along by the photographers themselves. Although the insecurity of the job was on a par with that of the times, it is only through the work of those traveling photographers—anonymous, unpretentious, and overlooked though they are—that the reality of those years of penance can be understood.[31]

The middle classes of the Franco regime and the new social elite that grew out of the need for essential goods and services were quickly superseding the bourgeoisie of the prewar years. The demand for portraits by these new political and financial classes increased business for traditional photographic studios and placed on a secure footing photographers who, like Jalón Ángel, Marín, and Gyenes, saw that they must establish themselves in the political and economic climate of the time.

The growing demand for portraits brought about a new golden age for photographic studios, which proliferated in Spanish towns and cities. According to figures in the Bailly-Bailliere yearbooks, there were 79 photographic studios in Madrid in 1949, 120 in 1950, 198 in 1958, and 231 in 1968. In the Calle de la Montera alone there were 15 studios, and 10 in Gran Vía. In Barcelona, concentrations of photographic studios sprang up in such streets as the Calle de Pelayo, where up to 10 portrait photographers were based in 1950.

As in the golden age of studio portrait photography, pleasing the customer was the photographers' first priority; this was more important than producing good portraits, if, that is, there were among these photographers any that were capable of such quality. "I learnt the freedom to be creative," said Gyenes, "and the knack of making people feel good. How? It is very simple: always show the subject in a favorable light."

Guided by this principle, portrait photographers adopted the decadent manner of the great prewar masters, who over-exploited hazy lighting and unfocused shots, effects produced by the large-scale cameras that were used well into the 1960s. The old 18 x 24 Globus cameras were replaced in about 1950 by the 9 x 12

Linhof cameras, Anaca cameras, and others, like the Plaubel "Peko" and the Técnica Jordan, also 9 x 12. Another development was that studios were now filled with elaborate sets, with real furniture, and ornaments that were perfectly in keeping with the taste of the European bourgeoisie of the 1930s. Alfonso Sánchez Portela fitted up his studio in Madrid's Gran Vía with a neoclassical staircase and a backcloth sprinkled with gold and silver dust.

Aiming to break away from his subjects' hidebound attitude, he built a full-scale mock-up of the cloister of the monastery of Las Huelgas; this setting was ideal for wedding, first communion, and christening photographs. Going one step further, Alfonso, as the studio was known, offered customers the opportunity to pose in front of a wooden staircase based on those seen in American musicals, painted white with simulated marble veining. Behind it the photographer hung a backcloth of damask and large, richly-colored curtains that produced a limitless setting for all manner of decorative props.

Portrait photographers would use such a collection of accessories in an almost endless range of religious or secular scenes, in which featured pianos, real or imitation chimney pieces, ornaments of artificial luxury, copies of classic works, and anything that contributed to creating the illusion of the bourgeois or aristocratic surroundings that would emphasize the subjects' social standing. Other photographers, such as Amer-Ventosa, thought nothing of photographing their most distinguished clients in their own homes. Meanwhile, in about 1965, Pérez de León fitted his studio with an overhead projector, which he used to significant effect in some of his famous portraits of female cabaret stars.

In about 1950, color film began to be used in photographic studios. Jalón Ángel, one of its strongest advocates, gave many courses on the use of color in his studio in Zaragoza and in other towns in Spain. Trained by Agfa-Gevaert and Valca, he began to use color in 1954, and in 1956 set up correspondence courses.

Manuel Coyne, José Cartagena, Juan María Ardizone (Kaulak), Schommer Koch, Sigfrido Koch, Portillo, Manuel Ferrol, Josep Masana, Pepe Gracia, Jaime Belda, José Casáu, Lafuente, Carlos Calleja, and other well-known portrait photographers were quick to take up color photography, although few knew how make full use of it.

Some of the most famous studios of the postwar period, including those of Cartagena, Derrey, Garay, and Kaulak, founded in the early years of the 20th century, had already become highly respected in the 1920s and 1930s, and a considerable number of portrait photographers had worked for the new regime during the years of the military rebellion. Among them was the Aragonese photographer Jalón Ángel, who produced a series of sugary portraits of Nationalist Movement members, presented in an album significantly entitled Forjadores del Imperio (Those Who Shaped the Empire). Very much in the mold of the traditional and uninspired style of photographic academism of the time, those portraits were instrumental in creating the new regime's official iconography. If Jalón Ángel never became General

UTRILLA. School photograph of Virginia and Josefina. Casasimarro, 1955. (Private collection)

OTHO LLOYD. Portrait of Eugenio d'Ors. 1942. (Salvador Martínez Collection)

JALÓN ÁNGEL. Postcard with equestrian portrait of General Franco. 1938.

ALFONSO SÁNCHEZ PORTELA. Colonel Moscardó among the ruins of the Alcázar of Toledo. 1942. (Private collection)

Franco's official portrait photographer, he was certainly one of his favorites, and he took official portraits of Franco from the time of the Civil War up until summer 1956. These appeared on posters and stamps, and were seen everywhere on the walls of barracks and schools, police stations, prisons, and hospitals. Jalón Ángel enjoyed enormous success, becoming one of the most sought-after portrait photographers, not only among Aragonese high society but throughout Spain. It is estimated that in his 50-year career, he produced some 50,000 portraits, most of them taken after 1939.[32]

Jalón Ángel's social and professional prestige was equalled only by the historic firm of Amer-Ventosa. Amer was already a recognized portrait photographer in the years of the Spanish Republic, during which he ran as many as four separate studios in Madrid. In 1944 he destroyed his photographic archive and transferred the business to his assistant Francisco Ventosa, with whom he set up another studio, which quickly became the most popular in the capital. Amer-Ventosa's portraits are typically sickly sweet, in a style that is midway between the old Victorian style of portraiture and a kind of secondhand Hollywood glamor that is nothing more than a pale imitation of the work of Cecil Beaton, Erna Lendvai-Sirksen, or Yousuf Karsh.

Respectable society in the Franco years held Juan Gyenes as another favorite photographer. A Hungarian by birth, he arrived in Madrid in 1940, with the benefit of a nebulous past that conveniently set the stage for him to construct his own legend. After working for a few years with José Demaría López (Campúa junior), he set up his own studio in 1948, and quickly attracted a well-heeled clientele. "I portray women as they wish to be seen," he said, paraphrasing the famous Karsh. This was thanks to his talent for flattery, his ability to dazzle the capital's social elite with his dubious and complacent art, and his ability to eliminate wrinkles, unsightly bulges, and other imperfections by retouching or by the clever but decidedly *passé* use of evanescent light. But if, in the grandly appointed rooms of his studio, Gyenes ever managed to take a respectable photograph, he was otherwise an affected, undistinguished, decidedly vulgar photographer.

The case of Alfonso Sánchez Portela illustrates the cultural climate of the time. Having reached top form after the Civil War, he set up a new studio in Madrid's Gran Vía, producing portraits of the major players in the Franco regime. These formed the corpus of an exhibition in December 1944. This was a cunning publicity move on the part of a man who demanded the right to make a career of his trade in a city gripped by memories of the past.[33] Alfonso soon regained his professional prestige. In 1949 he exhibited his famous

AMER-VENTOSA. The Spanish royal family. 1950s. (Biblioteca Nacional, Madrid)

JALÓN ÁNGEL. Official portrait of General Franco. 1950s.

photographic caricatures, one of his rare and modest contributions to the genre.

Nicolás Muller, who became established in Madrid in 1947, possessed both a rare ability to penetrate the character of his subjects and an extraordinary technical skill, qualities that quickly made him one of the most respected portrait photographers of his time. Muller's studio, like those old studios earlier in the century, was also a dive and a meeting place for liberal-minded intellectuals and artists associated with the Revista de Occidente. But Muller did not restrict himself to the four walls of his studio; on more than one occasion he used street settings for some of his most memorable portraits.

Other notable portrait photographers were Manuel, Ventura, and Cartagena. Manuel was among those who enjoyed the greatest success in the Madrid of the 1940s and 1950s. His studio was frequented by the most prominent figures in the government, the army and the financial world and, in almost 30 years, he produced around 30,000 portraits. In 1950, the photographers working in Cartagena's studio were Leopoldo Carta-

gena, founder of the dynasty, his son José Cartagena Pelegrín, and his grandson José Cartagena López-Carrión. This studio, the frequent meeting place of Perico Chicote, Mariano Benlliure, Jacinto Benavente, Muñoz Seca, and Tomás Borrás, was staffed by up to 12 people, although this figure was substantially reduced by the crisis that began in about 1960. In reaction to the circumstances, José Cartagena López introduced color in 1956, and gradually extended his range to cover decorative work, fashion, advertising, and the teaching of photography, creating the Escuela de Fotografía Profesional in 1961.

In 1951, at a prodigiously early age, Vicente Ibáñez, the youngest member of a family of photographers that went back to the age of the *carte-de-visite*, set up a studio in Madrid's Gran Vía. A man of great professional integrity, Ibáñez emphatically spurned the classic courtly photographic portrait, typified by refined composition and bold lighting, and faces shown in shadow. He soon joined the ranks of fashionable photographers and was sought out by Madrid's young actors and singers, who became the subjects of more

than 1,500 portraits that he produced between 1955 and 1970. Such was the success of his studio that he employed as many as eleven staff, including accountants, laboratory technicians, and retouchers.

The 1940s and 1950s were also a favorable time for portrait photography in Barcelona, although in those years of excessive centralization studios in that city never attained the popularity of those in Madrid. Most of the best-known studios were located in the Calle Pelayo, and in 1950 as many as ten were in business there. Prominent among them were the studio known as Napoleón and those run by Meyer, Boiada, and Navarro, some of which had a distinguished professional lineage. Barcelona's other notable portrait photographers included Guirau, Lucas, Ramón Batlles, and Josep Compte. For years Compte worked with Ramón Batlles, a photographer whose reputation was made at the 1929 World's Fair and who had worked for Agfa in Berlin from 1936 to 1938.

Despite the fact that both of them also worked as press photographers—they were two of the few photographers who were permitted to work in the streets—they concentrated mainly on advertising, fashion, and studio portrait photography. Sadly, because their archives were destroyed, very little of their work is known. Other great portrait photographers who worked in Barcelona were M. Duart, who had worked with Suñé and who inherited his specialty of colored photo-miniatures. The work of Pau Barceló, who was purged by the Franco government, was of a different nature. He ended up working as a freelance photographer and was expressly forbidden to sign his work. From 1960 he specialized in show-business photography.

In Valencia the busiest studios in the postwar years were those of Plá, Derrey, and Sanchís, all of whom had a distinguished lineage. Plá was established in 1862 by Valentín Plá Marco, who was succeeded by his son Valentín Plá Alviach, and by his grandson Valentín Plá Talens, the best known and most highly regarded of the dynasty. Plá Talens, who ran a studio until 1985, became official portrait photographer to Valencia's middle classes. Derrey was set up by Jules Derrey in 1860. In 1892 it passed to Francisco Gimeno, one of Plá's main rivals in the 1940s. The firm of Sanchís was formed in 1908 by Francisco Sanchís Muñoz, assistant to the famous Antonio García. Today, the business continues under his grandson Antonio Sanchís.

The fashion for portrait photography was not restricted to the major cities. Murcia enjoyed the services of Mateo, Almagro, and Miguel Herrero, who produced *Fotos-Jerárquicas*, a collection of photographs comprising portraits of the major and minor figures of the province. In San Sebastián there were Pascual Marín and Sigfrido Koch Bengoechea; in Vitoria, Schommer Koch, who was succeeded by his son Alberto Schommer; in Cartagena, Casáu; in Pontevedra, Joaquín Pintos; in Pamplona, Pedro Mari Irurzun and José Galle; in Zaragoza, Manuel Coyne; in Huelva, Diego Calle; in Cádiz, Reymundo; in Málaga, Arenas; in Córdoba, José León and the company formed by José Jiménez and Francisco Linares; in Salamanca, Cándido Ansede and Gombáu; in Bilbao, Vicente Garay; in Albacete, Jaime Belda; in Ciudad Real, Vicente Rubio and Eduardo Matos; in Toledo, Rodríguez; in León, Pepe Gracia; in La Coruña, Blanco; in Santiago de Compostela, Luis Ksado; and in Vigo, Pacheco.

Prominent among these is Pedro Mari Irurzun, whose work was consistently imbued with great insight and a sense of style. The interest of his portraits, which stand midway between the formalist tendency and what Carlos Cánovas has described as an admiration for or devotion to his subjects, lies chiefly in their lighting and composition, especially when he moved away from the pictorialist pretensions of some of his early work,

LUIS PÉREZ DE LEÓN.
Portrait of the cabaret star
Addy Ventura. 1965.
(Pérez de León Archive)

exampled by *Melancholy* (1945) or *Nightmare* (1950).

In the final years of the 1960s, however, the traditional studio portrait began to suffer an irreversible crisis. The ten studios on Barcelona's Calle Pelayo were abruptly reduced to three, and the same happened in Madrid, in such classic photographic enclaves as Calle Montera and Gran Vía, where the studios of Cartagena, Juan and Vicente Ibáñez and Rodrígues barely managed to maintain a foothold in a climate devoid of the buzz of activity of the 1950s and 1960s. The crisis affected not only the number of clients coming to the studios but also the demand for portraits on the part of people in the public eye. Although the causes of this predicament were diverse—they included a dramatic increase in the number of amateur photographers, a change in public taste, and the fact that owning a camera was becoming much more common—studio photographers as a whole blamed unfair competition and the entry of unqualified people into the profession.

Manuel Aumente describes the predicament of the photographic studios: "The difficulties that the studios are experiencing are widely recognized because the general public use them less and less. Everyone knows that those studios have seen a dramatic reduction in the

number of their customers. A very difficult future for this particular genre of photography is therefore plain to see."[34]

Those difficulties had a bearing not only on the portraits of the studios' traditional clientele but also on those of actors, singers, bullfighters, and other people in the public eye. The television age, and the focus of advertising executives and publishing consultants, were turning photography into the province of a younger generation of professionals, who did not run studios open to the public, and whose style was closer to that of fashion and advertising photography in the rest of Europe.

Some of the most notable of this generation, such as Pomés, Miserachs, Maspons, Schommer, Masats, Forcano, Colita, and Toni Catany, had had a thorough photographic training and were familiar with the work of Sam Haskins, Guy Bourdin, Richard Avedon, Irving Penn, Harry Meerson, Chevalier, and Franck Horvat, who were then working for such influential magazines as *Vogue, Jardin des Modes, Elle,* and *Studio Vogue.* One of the pioneers was Juan Dolcet, who concentrated on portraits of sculptors and others who were involved in the plastic arts, bringing to these a certain formal daring, technical perfection, and powerful mood of introspection.

However, it was Alberto Schommer, the most popular exponent of this new style of portraiture, who dealt the final blow to traditional studio portrait photography. In 1969, Schommer, whose background was in painting and advertising, began publishing in the national press

his well-known series *Retratos Psicológicos* (1969–73), in which he steered clear of the austere style of such photographers as Avedon, Penn, Giséle Freund, or Diane Arbus and constructed self-consciously elaborate settings in which subjects pose with collections of objects that supposedly define them. In designing the scenery, directing his subjects' pose, and adjusting the scope of the image, so as to produce a theatrical and supposedly interpretative view of the sitter, Schommer resorts to an obvious, baroque symbolism, which also makes him a pioneer of portrait photography.

All this obviously implies a certain risk, in that the photographer may not always have an accurate perception of his subject.[35] Without underestimating this risk, which Schommer willingly takes, his great merit lies in his having successfully applied this formula to prominent figures in politics, the arts, and the financial world; these subjects, who are probably vain enough to be seduced by the opportunity of coming under the selective eye of the camera, nurse a secret hope of appearing in a better light as a result of this close scrutiny, which—it is fair to say—is not always indulgent or forgiving.

Among leading exponents of the new portrait photography Leopoldo Pomés stands out; his portraits, which are brimming with intuition, are pervaded with irony and complicity with the subject, an arrestingly exquisite appreciation of form and an unusually fine sense of composition. Irony, sensuality, lack of

inhibition, and a certain critical—and self-critical—disengagement also pervade the portraits of Oriol Maspons, whose photographs make up the surprising book *Animales de compañía* (1995). The firm of Colita also produced valuable portraits of figures in the Catalan arts world, which were shown in the exhibition *La gauche qui rit* (1972). María Espeus won wide recognition, after settling in Barcelona, in the 1970s. In her work, which was shown in the exhibition *Hola Barcelona*, her subjects—most of them people connected to the arts and entertainment world—appear to emerge from the image like a reincarnation of themselves.

Working with subjects from the same background, Toni Vidal produced a collection of excellent portraits between the late 1960s and early 1970s. Miguel Galmes, concentrating on the theater world, produced a series of portraits of actors between 1962 and 1964 that were later shown in the exhibition *Retratos del teatro* (1967). Portraits of Luis Buñuel by Antonio Gálvez are more closely related to a symbolism that bears surrealist and expressionist overtones; Gálvez is also noted for his collection of portraits of the Spanish and Latin American intellectuals who were living as exiles in the city of Paris.

Very gradually, with the mass invasion of photograph booths, which were introduced to Spanish towns and cities from 1963, the crisis that had hit the studios began to affect their traditional customers. That year, Tecnotron, the British multinational company—one of the four firms that distribute these machines in Spain—was alone responsible for installing 100 photo booths in Barcelona and 40 in Madrid. The end of the photographic studios foreseen by the old masters was nigh.

"The day will inevitably come," wrote Kaulak in 1910, "when the skilled, painstaking work of studio photographers is no longer needed, overtaken as they will be by the unstoppable advance of new technology and the interference of a large number of interlopers." Seventy years later, the old-established studios are, indeed, beginning to disappear—even Kaulak's studio did not escape—and today languish miserably, reduced to taking on work of secondary rank.

TONI VIDAL. Portrait of the painter Antoni Tàpies. 1969. (Photographer's collection)
EUGENIO FORCANO. Portrait of the writer Josep Plá. 1967. (Photographer's collection)

THE LAW OF SILENCE

The impoverishment of Spanish cultural life in the postwar years was especially reflected in the press. Whereas during the Republic 2,000 different newspapers and magazines had been published, in 1945 only 87 were in circulation and of those more than half belonged to the Cadena de Prensa del Movimiento. Circulation figures were extremely low, and distribution barely covered the major cities. Moreover, freedom of the press was restricted by the Press Law of 1938 and the so-called Fraga Law of 1966. The former was passed under the unusual circumstances of the Civil War, and was based on the fundamental premise that the press should serve the state almost as if it were part of the army. "With the Press Law," wrote Juan José Pradera in 1951, "the press, now suitably cleansed, became an instrument of totalitarianism, something that in the manner of a soldier joining the ranks served a movement that in military terms saved Spain."[36]

With the aim of "awakening in the press the idea of serving the state," as Serrano Súñer propounded when he announced the law of 1938, strict censorship was imposed and a School of Journalism established, in 1941, whose objective was to convert young journalists into true "apostles of thought and faith of a nation reconciled to its destiny." It was also impossible to work in journalism without being on the Official Register of Journalists; this was restricted to graduates of the School of Journalism, although the profession was open to those whom the authorities judged sufficiently patriotic to be worthy of calling themselves journalists.

For the same reasons, those who were considered not to support the new regime were debarred from working as journalists. Finally, the state took it upon itself to "check out the number of periodicals and their influence," keep a list of editors-in-chief, censor information, and make compulsory the inclusion of political slogans, editorial comment, articles, and photographs. So efficiently did this method of controlling information work that in 1943 the ineffable Luis de Galinsoga could say that for the first time "the Spanish press serves the state fully and exclusively."[37]

In this climate of repression and state intervention, Spanish journalists were subjected to a thoroughgoing purge, executed through the Public Responsibilities Law of 1939 or through the action of special laws like that of the Repression of Freemasonry and Communism of 1940. In fact, the purges had already begun in 1939; the mission of the powerful Comisíon Depuradora de Cultura y Enseñanza, run by the poet José María Pemán, was to play its part in bringing about the "jubilant dawn of the new Golden Age to the glory of Christianity,

SANTOS YUBERO. Uniformed photographers. November 1941. (Santos Yubero Archive, Comunidad de Madrid)

JOSÉ LÓPEZ. Attempted invasion of the Valle de Arán. 24 October 1944. (Zamora Collection, Mauthausen Association)

civilization, and Spain." Accordingly, universities, schools, and editorial departments were decimated. Purges were especially intense in cities like Madrid, Barcelona, and Valencia, where such important press photographers as Agustín Centelles, the Vidal Corella brothers, Díaz Casariego, Albero y Segovia, the Mayo brothers, Alfonso, Lluís Torrent, Pau Barceló, José Gaspar, and Puig Farrán, had worked. Many of them were forced into exile in France or Latin America. Centelles, Barceló, and Puig Farrán sought refuge in France and, having been interned in various concentration camps, found on their return a desolate landscape in which they were debarred from practising their profession.

The company formed by Torrent, Gaspar, and Sagarra was forced to close down. Torrent and Gaspar ended up in Uruguay and Argentina. Sagarra, meanwhile, watched the doors of *La Vanguardia*, the daily newspaper on which he had worked up to 1936, close in his face. The Mayo brothers went to settle in Mexico, where they established an important photographic agency. Díaz Casariego, Alvaro, Alfonso, and

Albero y Segovia were disqualified, and the same happened to various press photographers in Valencia, among them Desfilis, Finezas, and the Vidal Corella brothers. Other photographers and movie technicians, such as Francisco Boix and José López, went into exile in France. Boix was interned in Mauthausen concentration camp; the photographs that he took there were later used in evidence against the Nazis. José López took part in the invasion of the Vale of Ara launched by the PCE on 20 October 1944. Although not of any quality, his photographs of the offensive are a valuable graphic record of an important episode in modern history.

In general, leading Spanish press photographers were forced to leave the country, or fell victim to denunciation, dismissal, or purges. José Núñez Larraz, a respected press photographer who worked for *El Adelanto* in Salamanca, was debarred from his post by Juan Aparicio, director-general of the press. "I had just returned from exile," recalled Núñez Larraz years later, "and Juan Aparicio called me, requesting that I go to Madrid to see him. I arrived at his office and he didn't even let me sit down. As I stood he said: 'Your identity card.' He looked at it, tore it up, threw it into the trash bin, and told me that there was no place for me in Franco's Spain."[38] Disqualification also affected press photographers, like Santos Yubero, who could hardly be suspected of harboring Republican sympathies. A new photographic aristocracy thus came into being that owed its existence not to any professional merit but to the intensity of its adherence to the Nationalist Movement. So zealous was this control that in the early triumphal years the Dirección General de Prensa forced press photographers to wear a uniform, thus fulfilling the cherished dream of the ineffable Juan Aparicio.

Those press photographers that were most active during this period included the Pérez de Rozas, the Brangulís, Joaquín María Domínguez, the Merlettis, and Josep Compte, who worked in Barcelona; Santos Yubero, Contreras, Pastor, Hermes Pato, Olegario Pérez de Castro, and Campúa junior in Madrid; Juan José Serrano in Seville; José Cabrelles Sigüenza in Valencia; Hermenegildo Vallvé in Tarragona; Ángel Blanco in La Coruña; Cecilio in Bilbao; Pascual Marín in San Sebastián;

BOTÁN. *The flying bull.*
1973. (Botán Picture Agency)

BALDOMERO. Manolete
at an amateur bullfight.
Arganda, 1944. (Pepe
Aguayo Collection)

Federico Vélez in Burgos; and Jaime Calafell in Lérida.

Of these, it was Compte and Campúa who were the most representative. Compte played an active part in the confiscation of negatives from photographers who had worked during the war, and for many years Campúa was the only photographer at the palace of El Pardo.[39] These more or less official press photographers were soon joined by a heterogeneous group of professionals who were in charge of all visual information in the first decades after the war. In Barcelona, there were Antonio Sáenz Guerrero, who worked as a contributor to *Destino*, *Diario de Barcelona*, and *Mundo Deportivo*; Josep Postius, who, after being interned in Miranda de Ebro concentration camp, began contributing to *Diario de Barcelona* in 1942; Josep Valls Gili, Merletti's assistant, who between 1945 and 1970 worked with his son Josep Valls i Sorolla; and Pérez Molinos, who on his release from prison in 1941 worked with Martín de Riquer in the Jefatura Provincial de Propaganda.

In Madrid there were Contreras and Luis Alonso Martín, who worked for the agency Efe and contributed to *ABC*; Agustín Peña Vega, who specialized in sports photography; Vicente de Lucas Linares, a contributor to *Arriba* and from 1958 president of the Agrupación Sindical de Periodistas Gráficos; Hermes Pato, who set up the graphic services of the agency Efe; Rogelio Leal, who joined the staff of *La Actualidad Española* in 1953; and José Pastor, on the staff of *Arriba* since 1940.

In Seville Ángel Gómez "Gelán" and Serafin Sánchez Rengel joined forces with Serrano. In Córdoba the most prominent press photographers were Ricardo Rodríguez, Francisco Martínez "Framar," and also Ladislao Rodríguez. In La Coruña there was Alberto Martí Villardefrancos; in Vitoria, S. Arina and *Arque* (Federico Arocena and Gregorio Querejazu); and in Pamplona, José Fernando Galle y Zubieta and Retegui.[40]

Most of the work of these press photographers was undistinguished, weighed down as it was by progovernment routine, although some images by names such as Pato, Arque, Vallvé, Pérez de Rozas, Vélez, Martí Villardefrancos, Jaume Calafell, and Luis Vidal Corella were truly memorable.

In this context, bullfighting photography reached certain heights, thanks to such prewar names as

ANTONI CAMPAÑÁ.
Airborne on skis. 1945.
(Campañá Family Collection)

FRANCESC ALGUERSUARI.
Miguel Poblet in despair.
1962. (Alguersuari Archive)

Baldomero, Zarco, Serrano, Santos Yubero, Finezas, Gaspar, Valls Gili, Mateo, and Paco Sebastián. They were joined by the great press photographers who had come to prominence in the heyday of Manolete, among whom were Paco Mari, Arjona, Hermes Pato, Chapestro, Manzano, Luis Arenas, Rubio, Cuevas, Paco Cano, Fernando Galle, Daniel Gallego, and the Botáns, father and son. The Botán generation heralded a profound change in bullfighting photography, comparable to that in bullfighting itself. The telephoto lens was gradually coming into use, and those rough images produced by the pioneers were giving way to a more exact, more spectacular though less immediate style of photography.

However, the most profound and analytical record of the bullfighting world was not to be found in the work of specialist photographers but in the more subtle, closely observed images produced by such photographers as Catalá Roca, Leopoldo Pomés, José Suárez, Julio Ubiña, Oriol Maspons, Paco Ontañón, and Ramón Masats, who initiated in Spain the era of the great photographic monographs with his splendid book *Los sanfermines* (1963). Sports photography also took a step forward, thanks to the work of such classic

specialists as Ramón Claret, Joan Bert, Alvaro, Albero y Segovia, Luis Vidal, Zarco, Ortas and Luis Sánchez Portela, and Antoní Campañá, Pastor, Zarkijo, Agustín Vega Peña, Ramón Dimas, Jacinto Maíllo, and Francesc Alguersuari. Campañá, whose background was pictorialist, worked intensively for the magazine *Vida Deportiva*, where his assistant was Ramón Dimas.

Together with Francesc Alguersuari, they were the most distinguished sports photographers of their time. In the late 1950s and into the early 1960s a new generation of sports photographers arrived on the scene; Manu Cecilio, Horacio Seguí, Avelino Pi, Raúl Cancio, and the brothers Jaume and Josep María Alguersuari led a thorough innovation of the genre.

State control of information was meanwhile exercised through the monopoly of the agency Efe. It had been established in Bilbao in January 1939 as an official agency serving the regime, and its director was Vicente Gállego; it held a monopoly not only on political but also on visual information, through a wide network of contributors and correspondents under the management of Manuel Cortés and Hermes Pato. Notable among their team of press photographers were Carlos Pérez de

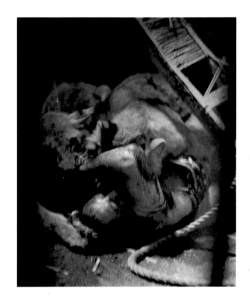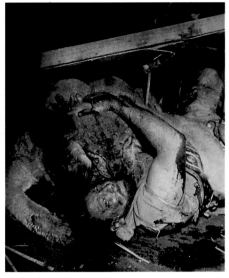

Rozas, Manuel Iglesias, Alberto Poveda, Olegario Pérez de Castro, Jacinto Maíllo, Luis Alonso, Ángel Esteban, Cecilio, Arenas, and Hermes Pato himself. In 1963 the agency installed its first telephotography line, which enabled it to tighten its monopoly on information. "In practical terms," wrote Enrique Bustamante, "this monopoly on information remained unchanged and, with controlled openings, beyond the approbation of the constitution of 1978."[41] With the foundation of Pyresa (Agencia de Prensa y Radio Española) by the Delegación de Prensa y Propaganda del Movimiento in 1945, state control of information was complete.

The agency Europa Press, which had close ties with the political and economic sectors controlled by Opus Dei, was established in 1957 by such men as Antonio Fontán, Gonzalo Fernández de la Mora, and Florentino Pérez Embid. More up to date and competitive than Efe, Europa Press was a picture agency which counted among its photographers José Hilario Cuadrado, Rafael Pascual, Paco Ontañón, Daniel Blanco, César Lucas, Antonio Alcoba, and Alejandro Peromingo.

News photography was also affected by the absence of the great illustrated publications of the previous era, such as *Estampa, Imatges, Crónica, Mundo Gráfico*, and *Blanco y Negro*, whose place was taken by *Fotos, Revista*, and *Destino*. This latter appeared in 1947, and was run by writers with Falangist sympathies, among them Ignacio Agustí, Juan Ramón Masoliver, and José María Fontana. Photographers who contributed to it included Catalá Roca, Ramón Dimas, Ernest Vila, and Monserrat Manent. Under the editorship of José María Vergés, *Destino* then became a real school of photojournalism and an excellent platform for such young Catalan

news photographers as Xavier Miserachs, Jaume Buesa, Eugenio Forcano, Pilar Aymerich, Colita, and Toni Catany.

The weekly *Revista* was also very important. It was founded by Alberto Puig Palau in 1952, as a competitor to *Destino*, and its ideology was inspired by the liberal Falangist sector, including Dionisio Ridruejo, Luis Felipe Vivanco, Eugenio D'Ors, and Luis Rosales; its contributors included Catalá Roca, who provided most of its cover images. The regime's major illustrated publication, however, was *Fotos*. Subtitled "Semanario Gráfico Nacionalsindicalista," it was founded in San Sebastián in 1937 by Manuel Fernández Cuesta. Early contributors to *Fotos*, which was printed by high-quality photogravure, were Pascual Marín, Campúa, Compte, Carlos Pérez de Rozas, Garay, Almarza, Manuel Coyne, Santos Yubero, Badosa, Luis Vidal, Quintana, Arenas, Videa, and Contreras. In 1940, it was supplemented by a Madrid edition, whose team of news photographers included Cecilio, Gombau, Zarco, Gyenes, and Claret. After some years of slow decline, it ceased publication in 1963.

The most prominent newspapers were *La Vanguardia* of Barcelona, and the Falangist daily *Arriba*. Those who worked for the former included members of the Pérez de Rozas family, Hermenegildo Vallvé, Bienvenido Suárez, Jaume Buesa, Antoni Campañá, Jaume Calafell, and other younger photographers such as Josep María Alguersuari and Toni Catany, who was associated with the paper from 1967 to 1969. In 1951 *Arriba* devoted eight photogravure pages entirely to photographs. Its contributors included Pastor, Luis Vidal, Contreras, Blanco, Cuevas, Cano, Salas Torremocha, Pedro Pascual, Basabe, and Zarco, of whom Contreras and Pastor were the most regular.

CÉSAR LUCAS. Ernesto *Che* Guevara in Madrid's university district. June 1959. (Europa Press Archive)

TONI CATANY.
Formentera, 1969.
(Photographer's collection)

The great illustrated weeklies, such as *Gaceta Ilustrada* and *La Actualidad Española*, began to appear in the 1950s. The former was launched in 1955 by the group Godó. Although it used a lot of agency material, it also featured the work of photographers of the stature of Catalá Roca, Luis Hernández Calderón, Oriol Maspons, Ramón Masats, Xavier Miserachs, Julio Ubiña, and the young Manuel López Rodríguez. Miserachs was simultaneously contributing to *Triunfo*, a leading magazine for which Ramón Rodríguez, Martínez Parra, Carmen Basáñez, and Jorge Rueda also worked. *La Actualidad Española*, with links to *Opus Dei*, was launched in 1952, and featured the work of Paco Ontañón, César Lucas, Rogelio Leal, and Antonio Navas.

But these were not favorable times for the great illustrated magazines. The type of photographs that appeared in the pages of magazines like *Vu, Life, Picture Post, Paris-Match*, and *Stern* seemed to be outpaced by the irrepressible rise of television. *Collier's*, the prestigious weekly, closed in 1957; in 1963 a group of news photographers led by Eduard Boubat left *Réalités*; in 1972 the circulation figures for *Paris-Match* took an alarming dive, and that same year *Life* ceased publication after a slow, unstoppable decline. In Spain the strength of television led to the closure of the best of the illustrated weeklies or to a serious decline in their circulation. *La Actualidad Española* closed in 1977, *Triunfo* in 1982, and, finally, *Gaceta Ilustrada* in 1984.

"Weekly news magazines," wrote Miserachs, "were eroded and destroyed by television; illustrated news, broadcast live or prerecorded shortly before transmission, emerged the winner, and the advertising that financed it found a greater return by investing in the small screen. This state of affairs came about almost simultaneously all over the world, and as a result the photographic staff of those weeklies were dismissed."[42] News photographers like Masats, Forcano, Ubiña, Maspons, César Lucas, Ontañón, and Miserachs himself had to regear. Some went to work for the daily newspapers, or for television; others joined the Sunday magazines that were beginning to be produced by the newspapers, or sought other work in the field of fashion, advertising, or publishing.

On another level, as in the early years of Spanish news photography, the work of photographers continued to be undervalued by editors. "On the borderline between the worlds of photography and journalism," wrote Manuel López Rodríguez in 1981, "the reporter with a camera has not yet won the battle for images in editorial departments. Being marginalized, those who provide visual news are given little space."[43]

Even when democracy had been established, Spanish news photographers lacked the right training, and few were qualified to work for newspapers and magazines. "Most of the time," recalled Juan Luis Cebrián, the first editor of *El País*, in 1980, "photographs merely illustrated the story, and there exists an objective neglect of graphic journalism in the dailies, perhaps feeling overshadowed by the overpowering strength of television. As far as photography is concerned, the experience of *El País* has been a complete failure."[44]

Nevertheless, and despite so many limitations and deprivations, a new generation of news photographers was to spearhead the most profoundly innovative movement in Spanish photojournalism since the time of the Republic. After nearly 40 years of censorship, control, and suppression of information, young photojournalists took up the old pioneering spirit, conscious of their civil responsibility in the common fight for democratic freedom. This new kind of photojournalism, profoundly engaged with its time, spoke a new, militant language; for example, Ben Fernández, Charles Harbutt, Jill Firedman, and Gilles Caron closely recorded the horrors of the Vietnam War, the Paris students' protest of May 1968, and the deprivation and violence that were rife in the poor areas of major cities.

The new photojournalism first became evident in those sectors that most actively pushed for democracy. The work of young photojournalists reflected the reality of a country committed to a long-drawn-out fight against dictatorship. Many of the events that they covered held obvious risks. Moreover, because they

DEMETRIO ENRIQUE. Procession at Corpus Christi. Toledo, 1970. (Photographer's collection)

GUSTAVO CATALÁN. Demonstration by the extreme right wing. Madrid, 1975. (Photographer's collection)

MANEL ARMENGOL. Political repression during a pro-amnesty demonstration. Barcelona, 1976. (Photographer's collection)

were freelancers and had very little job security, they were almost totally legally defenseless against firms and political and government authorities. The movement was in any case not homogeneous, and it was joined by young people with links to clandestine political and trade union organizations, by professional photographers who were bored with the routine of their work on newspapers, and groups committed to winning recognition for their work, and, occasionally, photojournalists with a recognized track record, such as Maspons, Miserachs, Colita, Ontañón, Jordi Soteras, César Lucas, and Pilar Aymerich. Certainly without setting out to do so, the new generation of photojournalists found itself making demands on three levels: the fight for democratic freedom, the desire to bring to Spain a fresh, more modern style of photography, and demands for better working conditions.

Because censorship was maintained into the first years of the transition to democracy, the pictures that young reporters took—scenes of urban alienation, demonstrations by students and trade unionists, political repression, demonstrations and revolts in the streets, in factories, and even in prisons—had to be published either outside Spain or in underground newsletters.[45] The Grup de Producció was founded in Barcelona in 1973; its purpose was to distribute these images and have them appear in the foreign press, and its members included such photographers as Francesc Llovet, Pere Joan Ventura, Xavier Celayaundi, César Rus, Francesc Simó, Jordi Parramons, Jordi Morera, and Pilar Viladegut, most of them associated with the underground PSUC.

This nucleus spawned the agency CIS, for which Paco Elvira, Manel Armengol, Josep Gol, Pere Mones, Pilar Aymerich, and Colita worked. Jordi Socias, meanwhile, had founded the Agencia Informativa Popular (API) in 1972. Similar concerns were launched in Madrid by Juan Santiso, Guillermo Armengol, the brothers Gustavo and Antonio Catalán, Germán Gallego, Manuel López Rodríguez, Carlos H. Corcho, and J. Luis de Pablos. Together with Pepe Encinas, Carlos Bosch, Sigfrid Casals, Quim Llenas, Lluis Salom, Jordi Soteras (father and son), José Miguel Gómez, Eduardo Rodríguez, Pérez Barriopedro, Manuel Hernández de León, César Rus, Fernando García Herranz, and, occasionally, Enrique Sáenz de San Pedro, Demetrio Enrique, Elías Dolcet, Shaba (Aurora Fierro), Pizzi Press (Jorge Rueda), Yeti (particularly Félix Lorrio), and Paco Jarque, these formed the nucleus of press photographers who instigated the renewal of Spanish photojournalism in the transition to democracy. Some of them joined Aurora Fierro and Jordi Socias, who together founded *Cover*, the leading photographic agency of the period of transition.[46]

CÉSAR LUCAS. Demonstration. Madrid, June 1976. (Photographer's collection)

Nevertheless, and despite the high quality of many of the photographs being produced, the Spanish press continued to undervalue visual news material. There were, however, a few exceptions, namely *Primera Plana*, *Cambio-16*, *La Calle*, and *Cuadernos para el Diálogo*, which all had excellent picture editors, including such names as Carlos Bosch, Victor Steinberg, Jordi Socias, Eduardo Rodríguez, and Manuel López Rodríguez.

Gradually, the new photojournalists joined newspapers and magazines that had been founded in the years of the transition to democracy; these included *Posible*, *Interviu*, *Canigó*, *El País*, *Tele-Express*, *Mundo*, *Primera Plana*, *Cambio-16*, *La Calle*, and others that heralded a new dawn, like *Cuadernos para el Diálogo*, *Destino*, and *Treball*.

But, although visual material had gained in prominence and photographers had a higher profile, press photography continued to be dogged even after the transition to full democracy. In 1981, during the Primeras Jornadas Catalanas de Fotografía, the Associació de Fotògrafs de Premsa i Comunicació de Catalunya, founded in 1977, denounced the neglect of visual material by the press, along with the insecurity of employment experienced by press photographers.

Those problems were to be compounded by other problems. These arose from the pro-government routine that followed on from the burst of creative enthusiasm in that fleeting spring of Spanish news photography that had flourished between the years 1972 and 1980.

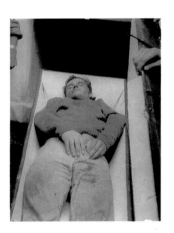

Juan Paredes Manot (*Txiqui*), a member of ETA shot in 1975. Photograph secretly taken by his lawyer, MARC PALMÉS.

CARLOS CORCHO. A member of the extreme right wing shooting a Carlist demonstrator. Montejurra, March 1976. (Photographer's collection)

THE ICE MELTS

The 1950s saw the beginnings of a thaw in the Franco regime. The purpose behind this was to shake off the burden of Nationalism and move closer to the neoliberal capitalist model. As the result of Spain's new economic orientation (designed by the technocrats of Opus Dei who were beginning to control government to the detriment of the shrinking number of Nationalist fundamentalists), Spain was in time to join the United Nations, the OECD, and the International Monetary Fund.

Between 1951 and 1957 national income had returned to 1935 levels; rationing also ceased and attempts were made to integrate the country into the world economy. The need to adapt to the demands of the new economic orthodoxy led to the government launching the Stabilization Plan in 1959; the implications were a severe devaluation of the peseta, rigid pay control, and a tightening of the economy that would allow Spain to join the European Union.

As a consequence, the number of industrial workers increased to the detriment of the rural and peasant population, and this led to widespread migration. Between 1961 and 1965 an estimated 900,000 people left the poorest areas of the country for the urban jungles of Madrid, Barcelona, or Valencia.

Likewise, between 1960 and 1967, the number of workers who were forced to seek employment in the economic havens of Europe easily exceeded one million. According to figures issued by the Ministry of Employment, economically assisted emigration abroad reached 1,742,428 people between 1959 and 1970, although authorities like that at Salustiano del Campo estimate that the unstoppable exodus was in fact 214 percent above given official figures.[47]

Spain was opening up: while floods of emigrants were leaving, tourists were entering. Whereas a total of 1,263 foreign nationals came to Spain in 1951, in 1970 the figure exceeded 24 million. The foreign currency sent home by the emigrants increased dramatically over the same period. Furthermore, the influx of foreign capital increased steadily from 1962, converting many of Spain's major firms into subsidiaries of the world's great multinationals.

The arrival of US capital was particularly important since the bilateral accords of 1953, and in the 1960s reached truly astronomical figures. The influx of funds was nothing less than a Trojan horse for a cultural colonization without precedent in the modern history of Spain. This cut even deeper with the invasion of television, which brought with it the neoliberal philosophy of the empire.[48] The omnipresence of Anglo-Saxon

JEAN MOHR. Emigrants at passport control. Geneva, 1972. (Photographer's collection)

culture, the large-scale migrations, and the influence of tourism meant the loss of moral and cultural models and points of reference, and sounded the knell for Spanish traditional life.

However, these profound changes in the country's economic outlook hardly had any effect on the political situation, due to the very nature of a regime still sustained by political repression and a total clampdown on democratic freedom.

In the field of artistic creativity, the 1950s were to be decisive. For obvious political reasons, and because of the general paralysis of all aspects of cultural life, the Spanish art scene—with very few exceptions—was scraping by on a miserable diet of national fine art exhibitions and autumn shows. Toward the end of the 1940s, dissident voices began to be heard, especially in Catalonia.

In 1948, a Salón de Octubre (October Exhibition) was launched, and the same year the group Dau al Set was formed; it comprised Antoni Tàpies, Joan Ponç, Modest Cuixart, Joan Brossa, and Luis E. Cirlot, with whom were associated such photographers as Joaquín Gomis, Leopoldo Pomés, and Català Roca. In 1957 two groups, highly representative of contemporary Spanish art, came into being: El Paso and Equipo 57 were headed by artists like Rafael Canogar, Manolo Millares, Antonio Saura, Luis Feito, Martín Chirino, Manuel Rivera, Pablo Serrano, and Agustín Ibarrola.

In parallel, painters like Zamorano and José Ortega proposed an art of denunciation that was deeply committed to reality, and a similar stance was taken by

JULIO UBIÑA. Traffic policeman. Valladolid, 1958. (Ubiña Archive)

The Family of Man

The greatest photographic exhibition of all time—503 pictures from 68 countries—created by Edward Steichen for The Museum of Modern Art. Prologue by Carl Sandburg

Catalog of the exhibition,
The Family of Man, 1955.

ORIOL MASPONS.
Nen d'Eivissa. 1954.
(Photographer's collection)

FRANCISCO GÓMEZ.
Bicycle inside a church. 1963.
(Photographer's collection)

musicians, moviemakers, playwrights, novelists, and poets who, in the words of Juan Goytisolo, turned their work into a "mirror of dark, humble, daily fight undertaken by the Spanish people for their lost freedom."[49]

Photography, still alien from artistic and cultural circles, and despised or ignored by them, remained aloof from that dialectical tension; although photography was thus spared the excesses of certain members of that generation, it was also deprived of its dynamism and of its innovative, iconoclastic, and multifaceted power. The framework within which photography existed had remained unchanged since the early 1940s. Political change, which had had a certain impact on other artistic fields, had hardly affected photography, enclosed as it was in the self-regarding world and puerile esthetic mannerisms of associations and exhibitions.

However, with the end of the dictatorship, regionalist and nationalist traditions lost their vigor, and the ideological justification on which many of neopictorialism's artistic assumptions were based were undermined. The policy of economic development of the 1960s also brought in its wake new cultural influences and new attitudes toward photography; these attitudes were being shaped by members of the international avant-garde who upheld social realism, whose defining moment was the exhibition *The Family of Man* in 1955.

Spanish photographers eventually began to question neopictorial academism, whose morbid influence was still deeply rooted in pro-government circles of the time. Radical objections—as José María Artero noted in 1958—were raised with regard to pictorial photography and *modern* photography; photography that "badly imitated painting" and photography "of our time." This meant nothing less than a return to the esthetic proposals that had been the starting point of the interwar revolution in photography, and which were repeatedly endorsed by such photographers as Paul Strand, Brassaï, Man Ray, and Catalá Pic, and which Artero emphasized more than 30 years later: "We do not want what we do to look like paintings: we want it to be photography pure and simple."[50]

Nevertheless, not having recourse to exhibitions, publication, or a market for their work, the only option open to photographers was the small world of associations and their exhibitions. The fight for innovation implied another, parallel fight against those photographic circles in which the old pictorialist academism was entrenched.

This struggle was not exclusive to Spain and was already manifesting itself in other countries. In England in 1950, such major photographers as Cecil Beaton, Bill Brandt, and Helmut Gersheim turned their backs on the Royal Photographic Society, convinced of the impossibility of modernizing an institution whose sole aim, as Gersheim put it, was to perpetuate an "antiquated, confused, sentimental, and saccharine" style of photography.

In Italy, photography had played a leading role in the postwar neorealist movement, through such alternative groups as La Bussola (1947), led by Giuseppe Caballi, Fulvio Roiter, and Mario Giacomelli; Misa (1954), comprising Giacomelli, Feroni, Bocci, and Silvio Pelegrini; and Friulano per una nuova fotografia (1955), headed by Fulvio Roiter. In France, the hidebound attitude of societies had provoked photographers like Jean Dieuzaide, Jean-Claude Gautrand, Georges Guilpin, and Roger Doloy to set up such influential groups as 30 x 40 and Cercle des XII.

In Germany the group Fotoform was created in 1949, with Peter Keetman, Wolfgang Reisewitz, and Otto Steinert as members. Steinert, the theorist behind what was known as subjective photography, advocated the photographer's creative freedom so as to produce creative photography, although "always using the possibilities inherent in the medium." In the United States, novelty was spearheaded by such figures as Minor White, with whom photographic creativity was to make the definitive break from slavery to pictorialism.

These developments were to have a decisive influence on young Spanish photographers, as were certain key books, for example *New York* (1956) by William Klein and *The Americans* (1958) by Robert Frank, and the traveling exhibition *The Family of Man* (1955), which had positively seismic effects in the sleepy backwaters of Spanish photography of the time. "That exhibition," wrote Xavier Miserachs, "made an enormous impression on me. What I suspected must exist was there before my very eyes. This was what photography was for, and I immediately decided to take it up. The exhibition catalog is to this day one of the books that I constantly have by me."[51]

But, unlike in other countries, in Spain the new photography developed within, rather than outside, the photographic societies, whose best-informed members understood the old reformist principle that something had to change so that nothing essentially might change. To this end, they did not hesitate to take control of renewal, with the aim of registering the inevitable change, controlling its rise and gathering its artistic yields.

One of the apostles of that renewal was Luis Navarro (pseudonym of Luis Conde Vélez), a member of the AFC, whose article *El momento fotográfico español* (1952) landed like a bombshell in the midst of photographic circles of the time. "Our art photographers," he wrote, "are old and have not known how to overhaul themselves…. They limit themselves to repeating once, twice, three times, 1,000 times, 5,000 times the same photograph of the same farmhouse and the same trees that were produced before them. Like the buckets of a waterwheel, they go back and forth, up and down, without ever shifting to a new axis…. It is a tragedy for someone to be before his time; but it is a greater tragedy for someone to live in the past."

A year later, he declared: "The new inspiration cannot accommodate antiquated modes of expression, nor new modes of expression that are not backed up with new inspiration…. We are moving toward doors that are being opened to us by a generation of art photographers, young people who can look with new eyes and who are now vacillating before the distress that a past epoch represents and the hope of virgin territory for all that they want to achieve."[52]

From the heart of the Real Sociedad Fotográfica de Madrid, Gerardo Vielba and Gabriel Cualladó led the renewal in photography in the face of the formal and con-

ceptual obsolescence that, paradoxically, was endorsed by the society itself. For these photographers, key influences were again *The Family of Man*, the books by Klein and Frank, and the work of Richard Avedon, Irving Penn, Frank Horvat, and Toni Saulnier, all surreptitiously discovered in publications that were almost unobtainable such as *US Camera*, *Photography Annual*, *Popular Photography*, *Vogue*, and *Life*.

"After taking a long, hard look at these pictures," wrote Gabriel Cualladó in 1956, "I understood that Spanish photography had ground to a halt and had failed to keep in step with humanity over the years. A series of rigid topics and formulas were, and in many cases still are, the basic principles on which those who go in for art photography base themselves. I have drunk from the same fountain but, convinced that I was following the wrong path, I stopped and now endeavor to follow the path of young, expressive, emotive, human photography."

"The secret," stated Paco Gómez in 1956, "is to do what you like and not what other people like. My photographs will be the better or worse for it, but what I say is that they are mine and no one else's."

Like Gómez and Cualladó, the new generation sought a style of photography free of the prevailing technical preciosity. Technique, as Maspons had already said in 1951, ceased to be the criterion on which art photography was judged. "I am not undervaluing technique," said Gonzalo Juanes in 1957. "In the

ALBERTO SCHOMMER.
Pretty woman. 1957.
(Photographer's collection)

Catalog of the exhibition of photographs by Otto Steinert, 1958.

GERARDO VIELBA. *Young athlete*. Alicante, 1966. (Vielba Family Collection)

Spanish salons everything hangs on technique, to such an extent that it drowns out ideas, if, that is, any ideas exist. The result is an artificial, monotonous, and self-satisfied style of photography." The action to take now was to "eschew all artifice, rhetoric, and symbolism in photography," and pursue simple style that is "deliberately low-key, by comparison with the ostentation that pervades photography in Spain."[53]

However, the road to renewal—also taken up by such peripheral groups as El Mussol in Tarrasa, Forat in Valencia and, especially, Afal in Almería—was not going to be clear of obstacles, and soon led to opposition from the most orthodox and hidebound sectors. It was not going to be easy to relinquish certain ways of producing "art" photography, ways that were so deeply anchored in the cultural and political framework of a system that championed artiness in photography over the documentary realism endorsed by the younger generation.

"Although in Europe," recalled Artero in 1991, "the particular language of photography was spoken and understood, in Spain we were still living in the 19th century; and documentary photography, capturing the moment, reflecting an instant's reality, was considered by some to be without 'pictorial' value, by others as a facile recourse to the 'art of the camera obscura,' and by others again, the most dangerous, as evidence of a latent threat to the social order."[54] This social order the censors and the zealous guardians of national values saw as threatening, when creative people—as Carmen Conde protested in 1946, in connection with *Nada*, the novel by Carmen Laforet—chose the "putrid, fetid, repugnant, and subhuman" as the theme of their work rather than the "creative, brilliant, and very beautiful."

Although photographers were still very distant from other creative circles (those of literature, the movies, painting, and the stage) and stood at a remove from their deep public and moral commitment, this incipient and timid rapprochement to "putrid and repugant" reality was fiercely fought by the big names charged with preserving the pedigree of Spanish photography. "Naked reality," wrote the ubiquitous Arcilaga in 1959, "cannot easily provide us with artistic material. Art almost always entails the falsification of reality, because only rarely is reality pleasant. It has to be embellished, idealized, polished, otherwise it can be repellent."[55] But, despite the opposition of those most orthodox and hidebound sectors, and the influence that the old masters still exerted—Ortiz Echagüe had just published his book *Castillos y Alcázares* in 1956—the bases of the photographic insurgence were already laid and firmly maintained by the most talented young photographers, who then set to work.

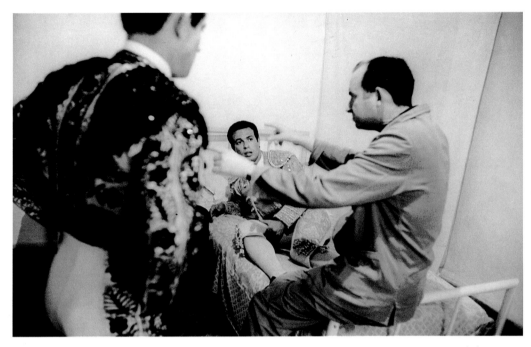

FRANCISCO ONTAÑÓN. *Curro Romeros' fear.* c. 1965. (Photographer's collection)

THE AFAL REVOLUTION

Although the winds of change were blowing through the heart of the photographic societies, the true renewal in Spanish photography soon went beyond the narrow ambit of their salons. In Barcelona, such photographers as Masats, Maspons, Miserachs, Pomés, Terré, and Ubiña were leading a secession beyond the bounds of the antiquated AFC, which was incapable of taking on board the new tendencies, beyond the so-called "modern" style of photography proposed by Luis Navarro.

These photographers, most of them members of the city's enlightened middle class, quickly became aware that the only thing they could bring to the society was a certain sense of unease. " 'Art' in photography," wrote Miserachs recently, "was its monopoly, and as we had initially suspected and were later to have confirmed, there was another, more universal and also more useful way of integrating photography into the cultural world. This created great inconvenience. Indeed, using the term 'modern photography' had been a euphemism by which 'art' photography, albeit of a more daring nature, could be accommodated within the status quo. Naturally, that was not what it was about, and that is why we ended up breaking with the photographic societies."[56]

During those years when the country was showing signs of turning against the dictatorship, Catalan photographers began to show their work. When Masats, Miserachs, and Terré exhibited together in 1957, this caused real commotion in the rusty cogwheels of the AFC. Leopoldo Pomés had exhibited at the Galerías Laietanas

ORIOL MASPONS. Apprentice bullfighter, from *Toreo de salón.* 1962. (Photographer's collection)

in 1955, capturing the attention of the city's intellectuals. In 1958, Ontañón, Cubaró, and Galí showed their work, the same year in which the Conversaciones de Fotografía y Artes Aplicadas took place, organized by Ramón Bargués, a talented photographer who met an untimely death. In 1959, Ubiña and Maspons exhibited at the Sala Aixelà and two years later the publishers Lumen launched the excellent series *Palabra e Imagen* with the publication of *Neutral Corner* by Ramón Masats and *Libro de juegos para los niños de los otros* by Julio Buesa. The series soon took in the work of Maspons, Ubiña, Ontañón, Miserachs, Colom, and Colita, with text by Ana María Matute, Ignacio Aldecoa, Caballero Bonald, Miguel Delibes, and Camilo José Cela, who were to play a leading part in Spanish literary renewal.

Lumen's publishing program and the vigorous activity of the Sala Aixelà, headed by Josep María Casademont, constituted a fine tribunal for those young photographers, whose work tended toward a documentary realism, indebted to the documentalism of Catalá Roca, French poetic realism, and the fringes of Italian neorealism. Between the magic of Maspons, the creative daring of Masats, the subtlety of Pomés, the intuition of Colom, and the analytical powers of Miserachs, this group, which with obvious impropriety was labeled the Barcelona School, wound up taking a decisive step on the one-way road toward the future of Spanish photography. This was quickly picked up outside Spain by such alert critics as André Thevenez, who had written the following in 1956: "A minority group takes its first steps and breaks from its petrified past, although there does not yet exist a real preoccupation with mankind that reflects the deep aspects of Spain. A certain optimism follows the times in which Spanish photography provoked our consternation."[57]

Ramón Masats erupted like a cyclone in Barcelona's photographic world, and the forthright nature of his work exerted a profound influence on photographers of his generation. He was the first to take up a pure, arresting form of reportage, with an outstanding collection of photographs on the subject of the boulevards of Barcelona. In 1955 he began work on *Los Sanfermines*, which was published in 1963. With this reportage, Masats abandoned forever the language of traditional photography, showing great freshness and creative power, surprising audacity in breaking current convention, and truly portentous intuition. By 1962 he had already published *Neutral Corner*, in which he reflects with overwhelming brilliance and a surprising maturity the sordid world of boxing, inhabited by shadowy figures who fight for their miserable patch of hope in the desolate poor areas of the great cities. After the publication of

JULIO UBIÑA. From *Toreo de salón*. Barcelona, 1960. (Oriol Maspons Collection)

Viejas historias de Castilla la Vieja (1964), Masats combined his photographic work with his interest in the movies and television.

Oriol Maspons brought a corrosive, demythologizing and critical element, cultivating every genre, including portrait, news, and advertising photography, and is also notable for the theorical work that he published in the form of dozens of critical and informative articles. His photographs, which brim with audacity, grace, and talent, always give a conspiratorial wink to whoever looks at them, and they have a hidden tenderness that, despite all disguise, is born of a moving neglect. Julio Ubiña, who was professionally associated with Maspons, had lived in Paris during the Civil War. He began working with Maspons in 1957, and together they produced *Toreo de salón* (1962). This magnificent book, full of irony and humor, is a piece of reportage without conceptual complexities, which speaks directly and has great narrative effect.

From his first works, Xavier Miserachs transcended the visible world to offer an analytical vision of reality, full of wisdom. However, he always worked within the

XAVIER MISERACHS. Rambla de Canaletas. Barcelona, 1965. (Photographer's collection)

GABRIEL CUALLADÓ. *Blurred children*. Pueblo de Castilla, 1958. (Photographer's collection)

FRANCISCO ONTAÑÓN. Boy with a pistol. Barcelona, 1959. (Photographer's collection)

bounds of a documentary mode that respects reality, staying true to his affirmation that in photographs it is not only the photographer that should express himself but also reality. Blessed with insight and a cultured mind rare among photographers of his generation, Miserachs was always conscious of the fact that time was in favor of his pictures. Those first pictures of his, which told of places, customs, urban landscapes, and the people of a Barcelona that is no more, were published in *Barcelona en blanc i negre* (1964). This emblematic book is a fascinating exercise in visual introspection into the life of the city through purely realist, albeit critical and revealing, eyes, and it is far removed from the apologetic and indulgent spirit of the majority of other such surveys. This analytical approach, full of hints and nuances, was to define Miserachs' later work. He also wrote an important theoretical work that is absolutely essential to the understanding of Spanish photography of his time.

The vicinity of Dau al Set is where the work of Leopoldo Pomés began, This photographer burst into the photographic world of Barcelona with images brimming with a suggestive and delicate subtlety. As Alejandre Cirici appositely remarked, Pomés is a great maker of dreams, a fecund creator of universes, of delicate formal balances. His photographs bridge the divide between fiction and reality, calling to whoever looks at them to indulge in fantasy, as far removed from gratuitous evasion as from the simple evocation of the immediate. Closely involved with audiovisual work since 1960, Pomés gradually moved away from photography to concentrate almost entirely on movie-making and cinema advertising.

Ricardo Terré, who shared Pomés' subjective vision, emerged on the scene in 1960 when he showed his work at the Ateneo de Madrid and the Photo-Club in Vigo. More than merely wishing to reflect reality, he wanted to transcend it. Through a limited range of subjects—death, ritual, or childhood—Terré tends toward timelessness. Obsessed by the semantic presence of death, he uses the most suitable technique to emphasize his own feelings before the inscrutable language of ritual. His images thus become real metaphors for his own interior world.

In 1958 Paco Ontañón exhibited some photographs that already showed his chosen vocation as a photojournalist. His language is simple, direct, without experimentalist pretension, but tremendously effective. Although he soon went to Madrid to work as a professional photographer, he has always maintained links with Barcelona, publishing through Lumen *Los días iluminados* (1964), a penetrating vision of Holy Week.

Colita, a photographic company founded by Miserachs and Maspons, and one of the Barcelona School's most typical offshoots, was also an all-purpose concern that encompassed portrait, press, and advertising photography. Their book, *Luces y sombras del flamenco* (1975), was the last in Lumen's series, and in it they demonstrate great versatility and a mastery of photojournalism.

Such photographers as Joan Colom, Eugenio Forcano, and Pedro Martínez Carrión were more closely involved with the AFC's activities. Fascinated from an early age by the sordid urban underworld, Colom always moved in the poor areas, more interested in the emotional impact that this world had on him than in translating this impact to unknown receptors of his pictures. His notable record of alienation in Barcelona—which he began in 1956 and on which he is still working with an obsessive tenacity—is one of the boldest, most moving, and fascinating pieces of work of any produced by the photographers of his generation.

Using a straightforward and surprisingly effective language, Colom produced a collection of photographs that echo his own interior reality but—as Maspons strongly pointed out—that remain faithful to the force and objectivity of the stark reality that he portrayed. A selection of those disturbing images was published by Lumen in the book *Izas, rabizas y colipoterras* (1964).

Eugenio Forcano, a photographer who concentrated on other aspects, is difficult to classify, his work occupying a position midway between pure photojournalism and the technical perfectionism of the AFC, which he joined in 1949. Receptive to the most wide-ranging influences, his talent as a photographer saved him from the academicist excesses of the time and from the excesses of his own inspiration. Contradictory and engrossed, Forcano had an undeniable range and capability, and is a small island in the world of Catalan photographic renewal.

Unlike in Barcelona, the new wave in Madrid began within the confines of the Real Sociedad Fotográfica, the star players being Gabriel Cualladó, Gerardo Vielba, Paco Gómez, and the Asturian painter Joaquín Rubio Camín, who had joined the society between 1954 and 1956. The works of Masats, who had settled in Madrid in 1957, had a strong impact on all of them. "Masats' arrival in Madrid," recalled Cualladó years later, "was decisive in that we photographers ceased to be members of the RSF. We were enthralled by his reportage on the *sanfermines* [the bull-running festival in Pamplona]. For the first time we saw work by a Spanish photographer that was on a par with that of great photojournalists like E. Erwit, W. Bishof, Robert Frank, Klein, and Cartier-Bresson. It was a real revelation for all of us,

The book *Los Días Iluminados* (1964) by FRANCISCO ONTAÑÓN.

The book *Izas, rabizas y colipoterras* (1964) by JOAN COLOM.

GONZALO JUANES. *Iron and steel industry.* Avilés, 1960. (Photographer's collection)

who were deeply bored with all the banality and mediocrity that surrounded us."[58] In 1957, Masats, together with these photographers, established the shortlived group La Palangana, which soon counted among its members Gerardo Vielba, Juan Dolcet, Rafael Romero, and Gonzalo Juanes. A few months later, Rubio Camín, Ontañón, Masats, and Juanes ceased to attend the informal meetings of La Palangana. Others, meanwhile, joined: among them were Fernando Gordillo and future members of the group La Colmena like Carlos Hernández Corcho, Rafael Sanz Lobato, Sigfrido de Guzmán, and Felipe Hernández Tarabillo. Between the reformist potential of the initial nucleus and the more ruggedly rebellious members of La Colmena, there developed a formal and conceptual synthesis that would eventually satisfy the dubious—and at times suspect—rural poetic that characterized the work of those members who thenceforth were to be known as the Madrid School.

It may be said that those who, on account of their background, seemed bent on maintaining the status quo of the RSF were in the end the star players of a movement of renewal; although it never went much further

than aiming to overcome, as Vielba put it, the "affectation to which modernism had fallen prey," the impetus did mean an honest drive to break with the puerile academism of the photography of the time. However, while Catalan photographers were always closely associated with Barcelona's most avant-garde artistic and cultural circles, those in Madrid—most of whom belonged to those sectors that best represented society under the Franco regime—remained entrenched in the inbred world of the RSF.

Isolated from the cultural life of the city, outside the artistic revolution and the ethical commitment of painters, writers, and movie-makers, the Madrid School of photographers remained tied to a mellifluous lyricism that in all too few cases transcended the romantic view of a hamlet, or the reflection of reality idealized by what passed as poetic vision: hence the almost total absence of urban or industrial locations in their work, which hardly lent themselves to idealization or poeticization.[59]

Nevertheless, having their own voice (in spite of its initial hesitancy), some members of the innovatory Madrid group, such as Cualladó, Gómez, Vielba, Dolcet,

JOAN COLOM. Barcelona, 1959. From *Izas, rabizas y colipoterras.* (Photographer's collection)

RICARD TERRÉ. Holy Week. Barcelona, 1957. (Photographer's collection)

Sanz Lobato, Hernández Corcho, and Gordillo, managed to break free of that limited creative environment.

Although Cualladó's photographs contain decidedly documentary elements, what they really shed light on is the character of their creator. Despite his declared admiration for Smith, his work contains none of the great American photographer's moral and humanist concern; it expresses instead the vision of a man who always aimed for simplicity and who very occasionally managed to transcend the personal world of relatives and children, and scenes and people from his emotional homeland.[60] In his work he takes a special interest in the irrelevant, the banal, the trivial, and the insubstantial.

However, the apparent simplicity of his images should not be taken as such; it is, rather, proof of their technical complexity and uncompromising perfection. This perfection is to be seen particularly in his portraits, in which without the slightest affectation he creates a nostalgic and mysterious world defined by a distinct and perfectly recognizable photographic language.

Paco Gómez's world is also a timeless and intimate universe where the incidental and anecdotal have no place. Immune to fleeting fashions, and conscious that honesty is the basis of all truly creative work, Gómez shut himself away within an enclosed and personal world, there to construct, honestly and silently, the austere and profoundly original language that he was to use to encapsulate the natural poetry of things—crumbling walls, scenes of desolation, graffiti, trash, tattered posters—of which Brassaï spoke. In this evocative, nostalgic simplicity resides the magic of Paco Gómez, the most forward-looking of the Madrid School, the most daring, subtle, and the most ironically tender and intimate. It is no accident that it was his work, together with Cualladó's, that most profoundly influenced young photographers in Madrid.

Juan Dolcet is a master of the well-executed work, the clear, simple, insightful photographic vision. He was an excellent news photographer and a great portraitist, and his work is both meticulous and gentle. He was one of the few members of his group to maintain an association with Madrid's artistic circles, and the one who was the most interested in urban and industrial locations. Gerardo Vielba was the group's great theorist. His dedication to doctrine and his extensive activities as a teacher, lecturer, and writer considerably hampered his own photographic work. But Vielba was a gifted photographer, who produced valuable, straightforward work that pushed at the frontiers of tenderness and ingenuousness though without ever managing to transcend them. With him, all was balance, and his are some of the most memorable images of his generation.

Between 1960 and 1970, Fernando Gordillo produced a sort of pious remake of Eugene Smith's *Spanish Village*. Deliberately avoiding any temptation to show "dirt and poverty," he tended toward an idealization that is indebted to pictorialist mystification. His express aim was to find beauty in a sublimated rural world, and he set out to create an idyllic and attractive image of rural Spain. Be that as it may, his valuable reportage on the village of Pedro Bernardo in Ávila province (without doubt his best work) contains some most outstanding images.

JUAN DOLCET. Plaza de España. Valverde de la Vera, 1958. (Dolcet Family Collection)

FERNANDO GORDILLO. First communion. Pedro Bernardo, 1969. (Photographer's collection)

Carlos Hernández Corcho and Rafael Sanz Lobato are two of the unsung heroes of the Madrid School. Corcho's vision is caustic and acid. He was the first to break with the honeyed, technically perfect approach of the RSF, opening up the way for other young photographers, like Sanz Lobato himself. Corcho later turned to news photography, becoming one of the most highly respected photojournalists of the period of transition to democracy. Rafael Sanz Lobato began working as a photographer in the early 1960s, concentrating on a systematic reportage of the people, customs, and religious festivals in the villages of Castille. In this sense, Lobato, along with Corcho, Dolcet, and Cruzado Cazador, was among the pioneers of anthropological photography, which was later taken up by some of the most typical members of the latest generation of documentary photographers. His enormous oeuvre has a fulsome solidity, and his respectful and comprehensive vision of Spain as it was in the 1960s and 1970s is among the most valuable of its time.

However, the most decidedly radical movement in Spanish photography of the 1950s was that which formed around the group Afal, led from Almería by José María Artero and Carlos Pérez Siquier. It came together informally after the bulletin of the Agrupación Fotográfica Almeriense was published in 1956, and its theoretical standpoint was total opposition to neopictorial academism and a forthright commitment to the social reality of the time. "We reject the aseptic, comfortable, middle-class stance of the happy medium," announced issue 4 of the bulletin. "We definitively support the photography of the time in which we live." "The photographer," stated Gonzalo Juanes in 1956, "can never feel himself alien to the vital problems of his contemporaries."

But, as Juanes himself pointed out, Afal never had the same commitment as other European groups such as Friulano per la Nuova Fotografia, which demonstrated a certain militancy as a statement of protest against an aggressive and unjust regime.

Neither could Afal take its rebellion much further, tightly controlled as it was by censors and government authorities. "We photographers did not want to go in for any subversive activity or strong social protest," explained Pérez Siquier years later. "The management would not have backed us anyway. In that historical climate, at the height of the military dictatorship, when our photographers had practically no civil conscience, that kind of committed photography could not exist. Authoritarian regimes do not allow artists to reflect their surroundings, and more than twenty years of repression were taking their toll."[61]

LUIS ZAMORA. *Milkmaids.* 1950s. (Centro de Estudios Fotográficos de Vigo)

Even so, Afal soon broke out of the narrow geographical boundaries of Almería. From the start, in addition to the tireless inspirational force provided by Artero and Pérez Siquier, Afal could look to Gonzalo Juanes, from Gijón, and Oriol Maspons, from Barcelona. Those four formed the theoretical and doctrinal nucleus of the movement, along with the incidental contributions made by Xavier Miserachs, Gabriel Querol, Cirici Pellicer, Roger Doloy, and André Thevenez.[62]

Its presence became so important that all the forward-looking groups that subsequently emerged in Spain claimed, with varying degrees of legitimacy, to be members of Afal. In this sense, it can be said that Afal was the most consistent, stable, influential, and forcefully secessionist of the photographic movements that appeared on the bleak cultural landscape of postwar Spain. It was through Afal that the most notable exponents of Spanish documentary realism became known: among them were Masats, Maspons, Miserachs, Ontañón, Terré, Colom, Paco Gómez, Cualladó, José María Albero, Cubaró, Jordi Vilaseca, Vielba, Pomés, as well as Carlos Saura, who soon gave up photography for the movies.

Carlos Pérez Siquier was one of the founders of Afal, and his work is among the most hard-hitting and original of his generation. From the social documentalism of his early work, Pérez Siquier developed toward a kind of magic realism that is deeply rooted in Mediterranean culture and which stands midway between analytical documentalism and a pure formalist approach. He later took this magical esthetic further, incorporating the surrealist and tenebrous elements that are to be found in his later work, which is purer and more concrete. Gonzalo Juanes is one of the most neglected members of Afal, and a major contributor in the realms of doctrine and theory. An admirer of Robert Frank, he shared the same sensibilities in that he adopted an inward-looking, subjective, and emotional style of photography. In 1963, his implacable logic turned him against photography, and he destroyed his negatives.

With a similar aim of overcoming the threadbare salonist esthetic came a young Alberto Schommer, who brought to the movement an expressive freshness and a readiness to experiment that was conspicuous in a milieu in which routine, crudity, and mediocrity were the norm. In his early work, Schommer avoided all contrivance, rhetoric, and symbolism—something that he was not always to do—tending toward a serene, daring style that contained no hint of the decorative. An extraordinarily versatile photographer, Schommer has tended to work in the most diverse genres, always with an enviable creative drive that is discernible in some of his latest work, such as *El Viaje* (1994) and *La Vida* (*La Habana*) (1994).

In those years of deep cultural and political depression, Afal's prominence was decisive in breaking Spanish photography's prolonged isolation from the international scene. This Afal achieved through its contacts with such groups as La Bussola in Milan, La Gondola in Venice, La Ventana in Mexico, 30 x 40 in Paris, Cercle Charleroi in Belgium, and Fotoform in Germany, as well as its participation in such major competitions as the second Pescara Bienal (1960) and the São Paulo Bienal (1961), and the exhibition that toured to Paris, Munich, Zurich, and Moscow (1959).

Such was the importance of this international presence that for many years Spanish photography was equated with the work of Afal members. "What I call Spanish photography," stated Enmanuel Sougez, the respected photographer and historian, in 1959, "is the result of Afal's efforts. So far has it come in the space of a few years that Afal now stands shoulder to shoulder with the most prominent European groups."

Just as the value of documentary photography was being questioned on the international scene, the move-

SANZ LOBATO. Procession in Aliste. 1971. (Photographer's collection)

ment was beginning to lose its backbone. Afal's bulletin, which the official authorities could never forgive for its independent and critical stance, ceased publication in 1963. Over time, its rebellious and dynamic spirit was distorted in the absence of a firm secessionist commitment among the great majority of its members, steeped as they were in the most conservative cultural and photographic milieu. "The form but not the content underwent a renaissance," wrote Maspons.

It then fell prey to a sort of documentary affectation that had already been denounced by Pérez Siquier in 1957. "I fear," he wrote in issue 11 of the bulletin, "that a superficial documentary style of photography will replace a no less vacuous salon style of photography." This new orthodoxy soon took hold in societies and salons, whose only care was to adapt to change so as to work it into their antiquated and hidebound vision.[63]

Added to this, a fair number of the most prominent members of Afal gave up their militant stance within the group to become professional photographers. The economic development policy of the 1960s, incipient industrializaton, and consequent broadening of the market, created a need for advertising, and this opened up new avenues to members of a generation that aspired lawfully to live by their profession.[64] In fact, certain members of the group—Maspons, Masats, Ontañón, Schommer, Miserachs, Pomés, and Ubiña—took up advertising photography, a specialty that they combined with their work as press photographers.

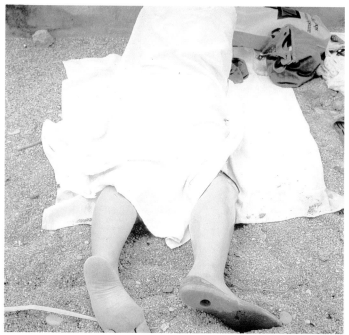

Others, like Gianni Ruggiero, José Luis Porrúa, the brothers Antón and Ramón Eguiguren, Toni Riera, Antonio Molina, Antoni Alba, José María Ferrater, J. M. Oriola, and César Malet, concentrated almost exclusively on fashion or advertising, taking up a branch of photography that had been established during the Republic by such people as Sala, Catalá Pic, and Masana, and which had hardly had the chance to develop a distinctive style in totalitarian Spain.

The absence of a tradition and lack of academic training were the cause of mediocrity in Spanish fashion and advertising photography, which contrasts with the work of European and American photographers of the rank of Richard Avedon, William Klein, Helmut Newton, Guy Bourdin, Irving Penn, David Bailey, Norman Parkinson, and Franco Rubartelli. However, mention must be made of the commendable standard achieved by Maspons, Toni Riera, José María Ferrater, Antonio Molina, and in the 1980s Javier Vallhonrat, the youngest, most brilliant and best-known Spanish photographer in this field.

Little progress had been made in other aspects of photography. The feeble reformist and secessionist attempts of earlier years having lost their impetus, Spanish photography was dragged into the mire of a new documentary orthodoxy, and few voices would rise to disrupt the routine of such a mediocre, limited, and emasculated outlook.

THE BIRTH OF THE FUTURE

Reaping the benefits of the international economic boom between 1963 and 1975, Spain had undergone development on three different levels that, in the twilight of the dictatorship, had resulted in the country ranking as the tenth world industrial power. Foreign currency brought in by tourism, the mass migrations of the 1960s, and growing industrialization maintained a healthy balance of payments, though the price was the sacrifice of traditional life in a rural Spain that was doomed and excluded.

This sacrifice (over 4 million people deserted their villages in the 1960s), the unequal distribution of wealth, and the fact that foreign capital was taking progressive control of industry represented the dark side of this economic development, which daily became increasingly dependent on the multinational companies, sheltered as they were by a regime that needed them.

However, economic development did not bring about a similar change in political and cultural life. The dictatorship kept up the systematic prohibition of civil liberties, endorsed by the most hidebound sectors of the army, the Church, and finance. Political repression stifled any kind of demand, as in the heyday of the Serrano Súñer Law.[65] It was in this climate that the strikes of the 1950s were organized, becoming more widespread in the latter years of the dictatorship and from 1969 leading to the declaration of successive states of emergency. Industrial unrest, fomented by workers' committees, finished by ruining the industrial unions.

Nationalist movements in Euskadi (the Basque Country) and Catalonia, meanwhile, were on the rise, and the non-Communist political opposition met in Munich in 1962 to work out political alternatives to the regime. The government's response to this growing civil insubordination was to step up repression. Distinguished members of the cultural world—academics like Tierno Galván and García Calvo, playwrights like Alfonso Sastre and José María de Quinto, novelists like López Salinas and López Pacheco, movie-makers like Juan Antonio Bardem, and art critics like Moreno Galván—were arrested and deported, while such occasions as the homage to Antonio Machado in Úbeda and the canonization of Sarriá, both in 1966, or the gathering of intellectuals in Montserrat in 1970, were politically suppressed.

The assassination of Admiral Carrero Blanco in 1973 brought the Franco regime to crisis point. Since the summer of 1974, political opposition had been intense, orchestrated by the Junta Democrática de España (set up in 1974) and the Plataforma de Convergencia Democrática (set up in 1975), which were made up of all the local parties, unions, and democratic movements. On 30 October 1975, the two organizations merged, demanding civil rights and liberties on a par with other Western nations. This was the end of a regime that, like its creator, was in its death throes in a climate of intense repression marked by the intensification of sentences handed out by public order tribunals and executions of members of ETA and FRAP.

In that context, Spanish art was strongly affected by the conflict that was raised to international level by creative tensions derived from the information crisis, and by the flowering of a strongly political pop art and new figurative art. The particular circumstances that defined cultural life in the final years of the Franco regime—the maintenance of censorship, the almost complete absence of an art market, and the strong commitment of Spain's most important artists and intellectuals—profoundly affected artistic output of the time. "It cannot be denied," wrote Valeriano Bozal, "that the relationship between art and politics was very close, although significantly, as occurred in the late 1950s to early 1960s, this did not lead to a deterioration of artistic standards. On the contrary, it acted as a spur, a catalyst, not only idealistically but also stylistically."[66]

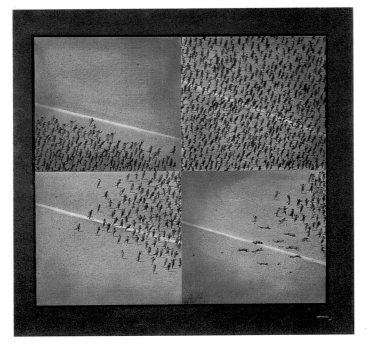

GENOVÉS. *Four stages in a political crackdown.* 1966.

The magazine *Nueva Lente*, number 84.

As before—indeed, as always—Spanish photographers remained aloof from those dialectical tensions, immured as they were in a new documentary orthodoxy, or barricaded behind the suspect alibi of the "revolution of values," to which clung certain of the most innovative sectors that grew out of the so-called creative photography of the 1970s. Photography also featured in the work of some of the most prominent plastic artists of the Spanish artistic avant-garde, who used it as a tool with which to denounce the repression of the Franco regime.

Among painters, Rafael Canogar was one of those who most often used photography, just as pop art was coming onto the scene in 1974. So intense was his relationship with photography that many critics labeled his work true "social reportage."[67] Genovés also used the medium of photography in many of his best-known works of the early 1970s, in which people appear as defenseless, harassed figures, deprived of all individuality.

In a similar vein, members of Equipo Crónica, like those artists who endorsed art engagé, produced what Tomás Llorens has defined as a documentary poetic, through which they emphasized the horror, the suffering, and the anger at a state of being disfigured by the repressive survival of the dictatorship. Ràfols Casamada and Alfredo Alcaín began to use photographs in 1963, and Romà Vallés, Antoni Clavé, and Modest Cuixart produced disturbing photo-

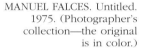

MANUEL FALCES. Untitled. 1975. (Photographer's collection—the original is in color.)

ELÍAS DOLCET. *Girl before the crowd.* Photomontage, 1973. (Photographer's collection—the original is in color.)

montages. Antonio Saura, meanwhile, gave up photography to produce his "stories," self-portraits, and bullfighting scenes that were to have such an influence on the later photomontages of Antonio Gálvez.

However, Spanish photography of the time shared little of the obsession and creative commitment of the plastic arts. From Afal's dying embers had risen a new documentary orthodoxy, exactly as Pérez Siquier and Oriol Maspons had announced in their day. Moreover, the lack of professional scope in the field of reportage, fashion, and publicity, the dearth of opportunities for exhibiting, selling, or publishing work, and the total absence of photographic collections in museums and other cultural institutions meant that photography was limited to the enclosed world of competitions and the moribund activities of societies. In that desolate environment appeared the magazine *Nueva Lente*, launched in 1971. Although it had few resources and in spite of its ideological inconsistency and its contradictory and confused eclecticism, it was able to home in on the profound desire for change that was the inspiration of a younger generation.

Held by many to be the mother of all avant-garde movements in Spanish photography, *Nueva Lente* did not attempt to be a local version of the British and American alternative movements that embraced everything: conceptual art, pop art, acid rock, and an underground culture of posters, fanzines, and pamphlets, seasoned with a dash of secondhand

Dadaism that was eagerly received by an iconoclastic generation whose only aspiration seemed to be experimentation and provocation. Young photographers who identified with the spirit of the magazine were distinguished by their eagerness for foreign prototypes, which they could use to take a stand against the routine foisted on them by the most conservative and hidebound redoubts of Spanish photography.

This readiness to assimilate and plagiarize generated a keen creative activity, as enthusiastic and prolific as it was confused, vacuous, and superficial. But what was lacking in terms of talent, what that plagiarism seemed to indicate, was a kind of demonstration of culture and even a new kind of esthetic for that generation that believed it embodied the essence of modernity and progress, and that was seduced, as Eduardo Subirats has pointed out, by the "rhetoric of a politically tamed and neutralized avant-garde, and formally defined by the most servile mimicry of models previously sanctioned by international criticism."[68]

Consequently, one of the distinctive characteristics of *Nueva Lente* was its militant apoliticism, in those convulsed and bloody years at the close of the dictatorship. In the opinion of its most prominent protagonists, the so-called "subversion of values," vaguely proposed by the magazine, was unnecessary in the context of the immediate political and social situation. As Pablo Pérez Mínguez said later: "We were above politics. Ours was an anarchist publication. You had to read the image by looking beyond the obvious. Our attitude was nearer to Dadaism than to political pamphleteering."[69] *Nueva Lente*'s other traits—especially in its early days—were its total negation of the work of the earlier generation of photographers, and a vigorous rejection and violent break with the immediate past in photographic terms.

From its first issue, the magazine's creators decided to draw a firm line between the past and a future that they themselves were to build by the so-called revolution that they were bringing about through its pages. "A naively mistaken attitude," wrote Enric Mira, "that springs from a lack of knowledge of the past history of Spanish photography. This points up the intellectual poverty of the arid cultural environment of the early 1970s, which was incapable of stimulating investigation and, therefore, the recognition of this historical past."[70]

However, not everything was homogeneous and straightforward in so eclectic a publication as *Nueva Lente*. In its first phase (1971–75), Carlos Serrano (who was in charge of the excellent design that was surely the best part of the magazine) and Pablo Pérez Mínguez were an important presence; the magazine was completely without ideology, was markedly eclectic, and adopted a naively provocative attitude that took the bankruptcy of reality as photographic material. The most eminent apostle of this doctrine was Pablo Pérez Mínguez, whom Joan Fontcuberta described as representing the "fun revolution." He made irony and parody the essential elements of a photography that sidesteps social reality to plunge into his own private world; this exercise in narcissism is also seen in the work of Luis Pérez Mínguez. This first phase was essentially experimental and, under the wing of such authors as Christian Vogt, Duane Michals, Paul de Noiijer, and Bernard Plossu, produced images that were pretentious, self-regarding, naively ironic or absurd, and technically simple and immature. The most active photographers during this phase included Paco Roux, Antonio Gálvez, Elías Dolcet, Saturnino Espín, Juan Ramón Yuste, Paco Llovet, Luis and Pablo Pérez Mínguez, Jorge Rueda, and Cristina and Marigrá García Rodero. Also important was the leading presence, besides Carlos Serrano and Pablo Pérez Mínguez, of Vogt, De Noiijer, Michals, Plossu, the ubiquitous David Hamilton, and Jean Claude Gautrand.

Nueva Lente's commercial failure during this first phase led its publishers to take a new direction. The editor was to be Jorge Rueda, who after the ambiguity of the earlier period intended to make the magazine less pretentious and elitist, and cheaper and more popular, though without relinquishing its critical and "avant-garde" spirit. By contrast to the elaborate, "private"

photography advocated by Pérez Mínguez, Rueda favored a type of photography that was closer to the world of the unreal and fantastic and that used photomontage as its vehicle. The fusion of critical and creative work so appositely identified by Enric Mira, the subversion of traditional realism, and insubordination before political authority of any kind were to be a few of the defining traits of this new phase in the life of *Nueva Lente*, which, moreover, was starting to abandon the arbitrary negation of the photography of the previous generation.

With Jorge Rueda, *Nueva Lente* opened up a new vision that treated reality with irreverence and was indebted to Balthus, Delvaux, De Chirico, Magritte, Topor, and other members of the Pánico group, including Arrabal and Cieslewicz, and the sequential surrealism of Duane Michals. Rueda, together with Joan Fontcuberta, Pere Formiguera, José Miguel Oriola, Rafael Navarro, Eduardo Momeñe, Javier Campano, Carlos Villasante, Manuel Falces, the brothers Antón and Ramón Eguiguren, Elías Dolcet, and Yeti, were the most active photographers of this period, with Gómez Buisán, Roberto Molinos, Enrique Sáenz de San Pedro, Manuel Esclusa, Matilde Imberlón, Juan Carlos Dolcet, Marín Chacón, Alberto Schommer, Cristina García Rodero, and Antonio Sánchez Barriga.

JORGE RUEDA. "My sister's boyfriends." Photomontage, 1971. (Photographer's collection)

Nueva Lente, number 50. (Photograph by JORGE RUEDA)

Photomontage became the most widely used medium by young photographers associated with *Nueva Lente*, who were strongly influenced by the vogue that it was enjoying in Europe. Their work appeared in the monumental exhibition at Ingolstadt (1969), and included work by photographers such as the Germans Klaus Staeck and Jürgen Holtfreter, the British group Minda, the Dutchman Paul de Noiijer, the Swiss Charles Vogt, and the photographic compositions of the Pánico group, widely published in satirical magazines that took their cue from the French weeklies *Charlie Hebdo* and *Hara-Kiri.*

Obviously, photomontage found an immediate echo in the pages of the magazine, and was occasionally taken up by such differing photographers as Esclusa, Fontcuberta, Oriola, Jesús Roda, Elías Dolcet, the García Rodero brothers, Vila Masip, Yeti, Alberto Schommer, Antón and Ramón Eguiguren, Benito Román, and Demetrio Enrique, and in more systematic fashion by Jorge Rueda, Antonio Gálvez, Miguel Ángel Yáñez Polo, Pedro Avellaned, Manuel Falces, Esteve Palmada, and Salvador Obiols. So widely used was photomontage in the 1970s that it produced a new orthodoxy or, as Valeriano Bozal

described it, a new avant-garde academism that was soon taken up by and distorted by the most orthodox photographic circles. This astonished some foreign critics, surprised at this neo-Dadaist epidemic with which young Spanish photographers were so gravely smitten.[71]

Of the dozens of photographers who took their bearings from the pages of *Nueva Lente*, few have survived as photographers, most of them "hunkered down and forgotten after their brilliant mediocrity," as Pablo Pérez Mínguez and Carlos Serrano announced with foresight. On the other hand, probably due to the youth and immaturity of certain of its most prominent members, *Nueva Lente* was more a magazine of negation, provocation, and secession than one that promoted good photography. Those that managed to survive—Falces, Oriola, Fontcuberta, J. R. Yuste, Yeti, Cristina García Rodero, Esclusa, Forminguera, and Rafael Navarro—took some years to mature and find their own style.

As Fontcuberta pointed out, the members of the *Nueva Lente* generation today feel "ashamed" of their early images, and are conscious that "the best work would be some years in coming to fruition." The sole exception may be Jorge Rueda, who went on to produce his best work and who never ceased to be surprised at finding himself a member of a generation made up of photographers more than ten years younger than he was. Rueda's work is related to the tradition established by Heartfield and Renau; rarely is his insurgency gratuitous or vicarious but springs from pure rebelliousness, great creative integrity, and a surprising imagination. His photographic work—his photomontage as much as his reportage, a facet of his work that is often overlooked—constitutes a profound protest against the dull, the trite, and the conformist, and the values of Spanish society at the end of the Franco regime.

Nueva Lente's great contribution was its power to shock and its role as common ground for the various photographic styles that developed as Spanish photography was entering a new-age dawn. The magazine closed in 1983, a victim of its contradictions and of its own elitist calling.[72]

But *Nueva Lente* was not the only dynamic force in the changing world of photography of the time. Various factors were shaping a new landscape in those ten years that shook up Spanish photography. A dozen new galleries and exhibition halls opened, new magazines appeared, schools and academies were established, and the foundations of an emerging market for photography were laid, thanks to the efforts of such key figures as Albert Guspi, who opened the gallery Spectrum in 1973, and the Grup taller d'art Fotogràfic in 1975.[73]

In 1972 the *Historia de la fotografía catalana* was published, and the first Spafoto yearbook appeared, devoted to fashion and advertising photography. In 1973, the Coteflash yearbook came out, and the first Everfoto yearbook was issued. In 1974 the first issue of the magazine *Flash-Foto* appeared, and the multipurpose Photocentro space was opened in Madrid under the directorship of Aurora Fierro. A year later, the magazines *Eikonos* and *Anófeles* came out and, at the instigation of *Flash-Foto*, the first Congrés Internacional de Fotografía took place in Barcelona.

The same year the group F-8 (with J. Miguel Holgado, Fernando Manso, Miguel Márquez, Luis Ortiz, Justo Ramos, and Maria Ángel Yáñez Polo) was formed in Seville, and in Madrid the group Yeti (with Antonio Lafuente, Félix Lorrio, and Miguel Ángel Mendo) was established. In 1976 the Centros de Enseñanza de la Imagen (CEI) were opened, to teach photography along with the already important Institut D'Estudis Fotogràfics de Catalunya. The same year, Photocentro published a Spanish edition of the magazine *Zoom*, and FotoRad mounted an exhibition of the work of Ton Sirera, who with Ángel Úbeda of La Mancha is one of the most outstanding exponents of abstract photography.

EGUIGUREN. Nude. 1974. (Private collection—the original is in color.)

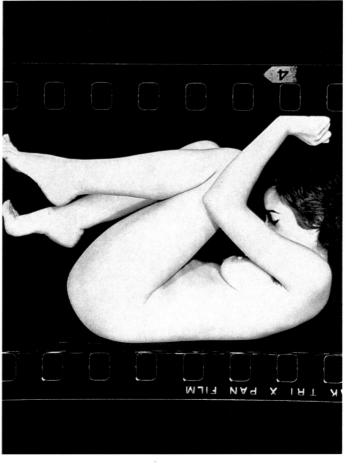

RAFAEL NAVARRO. *Involution-1*. 1976. (Photographer's collection)

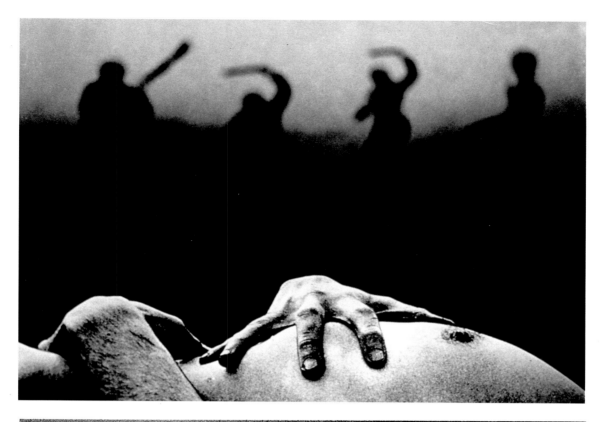

In the bloody close of the dictatorship, only certain photographers, such as Salvador Obiols and Jorge Rueda, managed to produce photomontages that made a political or social statement. Top: *Agressió a la pau* (1975), by SALVADOR OBIOLS. Bottom: *Our family* (1971), by JORGE RUEDA.

In 1979 the Centre Internacional de Fotografía was opened and the Jornadas Catalanas de Fotografía were held. These activities were complemented by many developments within the photographic associations (there was the Fotomostra in Lérida, and the Semana de la Fotografía in Guadalajara, the initiative of the photographic revival in Reus); these were mostly the result of the efforts of such photographers as Carlos Cánovas, Rey Cascales, Juan Antonio Duce, Pío Guerendiaín, Rafael Levenfeld, J. M. Ribas Prous, Antonio Tabernero, and Gonzalo Vinagre.

In that decade, Spanish photojournalism reached its greatest heights since the time of the Republic and Civil War. The work of press photographers reached a remarkable level, breathing fresh life into newspapers and magazines that had become atrophied through years of censorship, self-censorship, and limitations imposed by a regime that cruelly persecuted all forms of freedom, and most particularly freedom of expression. In the convulsed climate of the final years of the Franco regime, the life of ordinary people was faithfully reflected in the work of photojournalists of the rank of Manel Armengol, Gustavo Catalán, Carlos Corcho, Paco Elvira, García Francés, Germán Gallego, Manuel López Rodríguez, Félix Lorrio, Jorge Rueda, Jordi Socias, Pilar Aymerich, Juan Santiso, Eduardo Rodríguez, José Miguel Gómez, Pepe Encinas, Francesc Simó, and certain members of the previous generation, such as Jordi Soteras, Xavier Miserachs, Francisco Ontañón, Colita, Oriol Maspons, and César Lucas.

All these developments were to shape the future of Spanish photography, heralded in the early years of *Nueva Lente*. The secessionist and avant-garde tendencies, and the reverence shown toward the gamut of foreign culture that defined the magazine were not alien to the consolidation of certain tendencies in Spanish photography of the 1980s. The most purportedly creative of these tendencies cultivated a kind of neopictorialism that was more sophisticated and baroque than in its earlier manifestation, but equally indebted to the old Victorian view of photography as art, with identical inferiority complexes in relation to painting, and with the same lack of humility on the part of its creators.

This neopictorialism was born of postmodern confusion and the dehumanizing effects of post-industrial society, which meant the removal of all means of protest against power, the end of ethical utopias, the rejection of the old values of solidarity, the "joys of cynicism" and brave new media, all in the name of an economic development policy that would drive a complacent art market in which photography would ultimately take its place.

FRANCISCO JARQUE.
Untitled. 1975.
(Photographer's collection)

As in the golden age of pictorialism, the photographer once again feels the need to be and to feel that he is an "artist," which is the only way of breaking into this long-awaited market for photography that never came to fruition despite all the efforts that were made to achieve this. With this aim in mind, photographic materials were manipulated in many ways. This was to be expected of a certain post-avant-garde art that resorts to the most diverse range of techniques, defining an interdisciplinary creative process that tries to legitimize photography which, perhaps without reason, had been described as "illegitimate" art by Pierre Bourdieu.

"I refuse to define or frame my work once it is finished," stated Pere Formiguera in 1980. "Whether it is a photograph, a painting, or a collage. Really it does not matter much to me. I consider myself to be a photographer who manipulates his photographs, and when that manipulation is greatest a photograph can become a painting." In the same way that the old pictorialists used certain emulsions, young photographers find new ways of manipulating images to produce collages, superimpositions, seriations, montages, and photomontages, which are the modern counterparts of the various finishes that, as Brassaï described in 1932, the so-called artists of the camera used to alter the photographic appearance of their work with the aim of turning it into true "painting." But, although photographers manipulate their materials, sign and number

their originals and, in a pathetic case of submission to the norms of the conventional art market, destroy their negatives in front of a lawyer so as to guarantee the uniqueness and unrepeatable merits of their work, collectors and gallery owners continue to ignore them.[74]

The collective, militant spirit displayed by photographers in the 1970s gradually gave way to a marked individualism, which was only to be expected from the neoliberalism imposed by the mandarins of the new economic world order and their native executives. Photography was following the path of a creativity rooted in the conceptual, by contrast to the documentary avant-garde of the postwar years. Having declared reality bankrupt as photographic material, the photographer feels the need to "think out" or develop his images which, according to Duane Michals, would explore the "inner landscapes" of their makers. "It is no use going out into the street with your camera on your shoulder to see the world in a new way," stated Joan Fontcuberta in 1988. "In photographic terms, reality has had its day; we must construct new realities."

This rejection of documentary photography would spawn what Fontcuberta has called "contravisions," which imply a deep questioning of the very nature of photography as a medium in the mold of Cindy Sherman (a photographer, actress, interior decorator, and lighting technician), Anna and Bernard Johannes, Thomas Ruff, Milan Kunc, and particularly Jürgen Klauke, a distinguished exponent of conceptual art in

the 1980s, for whom the camera is wholly dispensable for the production of his works.

In other areas of creative photography, from the mid-1970s, a documentary current has swept through Spain, exemplified by the work of such photographers as Koldo Chamorro, Cristina García Rodero, Benito Román, Enrique Sáenz de San Pedro, Cristóbal Hara, Fernando Herráenz, and Ramón Zabalza, who have found themselves unable to deny the real world. By comparison with the "creative" photographers who favor developing or "thinking out" their images in the confined space of their studio, these photographers think of their studios as the world; they keep alive the old fascination with looking, discovering, and being amazed at the inexhaustible spectacle of life, and endorse Moholy-Nagy's affirmation that photography should be measured as much in terms of its human and social content as in terms of its own esthetic values.

Seeing photography as something that is done with care and humility, the new documentary photographers wish to be the honest recorders of the changing reality in Spain, at a time marked by the neoliberal economic apotheosis that is responsible for the destruction of rural life and of traditional cultural and moral points of reference.

In the context of this vanishing Spain, they wish faithfully to compile a record of its fiestas, rituals, and popular customs by means of a pure style of photography, and without manipulating their materials. Between the ethical commitment of such photographers

ENRIQUE SÁENZ DE SAN PEDRO. Franco's funeral. November 1975. (Private collection)

as Eugene Smith, Marc Riboud, and Cartier-Bresson and the documentary subjectivity of Robert Frank, they have chosen an interpretative and analytical realism, being conscious that subjectivity is, perhaps, the only sure way of reaching the threshold of an ever-dubious objectivity.

By the end of the 1970s, conceptual experimentation was showing signs of exhaustion and gave way to a subjective and intimate form of documentary photography that is seen in the work of Manolo Laguillo, Ferrán Freixa, Jordi Guillumet, Carlos Cánovas, Humberto Rivas, Manuel Sonseca, Eduard Olivella, Manel Esclusa, and Toni Catany. It represents a return to a pure form of photography, which reflects the melancholy and degradation of urban and industrial areas, and that is marked by formal perfection and a certain distance kept from the subject at hand: old commercial establishments, neglected buildings and landscapes, inner city areas, empty locations, deserted streets, uninhabited houses....

The 1980s brought a new sociopolitical situation, which marked the consolidation of photography that was fabricated or "thought out," and of new documentary currents, so tenaciously denied or ignored by the previous and devastating avant-garde. On another level, certain members of the Afal generation, such as Cualladó, Colom, Masats, Maspons, Miserachs, Ontañón, Pérez Siquier, Schommer, and Terré, have retained an appreciable creative ability. But, despite the undeniable vigor of Spanish photography and the recognition that it is beginning to receive in the world, its infrastructure in commercial and publishing terms remains practically unchangeable.

Only the dedication of photographers themselves—some of whom have sometimes felt obliged to become critics, researchers, and historians—and the beginnings of publishing programs and incipient patronage on the part of institutions and private individuals, have enabled photography to become part of the country's culture. In the 1990s, this phenomenon is finally beginning to become fully apparent.

FRANCESC SIMÓ. Clearing away symbols of Franco's dictatorship. Barcelona, 1976. (Photographer's collection)

NOTES

IN THE SERVICE OF EMPIRE

1. Fernando García de Cortázar and José Manuel González Vesga, *Breve historia de España*, Alianza Editorial, Madrid, 1994.

2. *Las Fuentes de la Memoria-II* contains two extensive chapters devoted to the analysis of Spanish pictorialism.

3. Quoted by Alexandre Cirici in *La estética del franquismo*, Gustavo Gili, Barcelona, 1977.

4. José Horna, "José Ortiz Echagüe: por el imperio hacia … la fotografía," in the magazine *Hika*, number 62, November 1995.

5. Joaquín Plá Janini, *La intervención en fotografía de arte*. Unpublished manuscript, 1939–40. Published in the magazine *PhotoVision*, number 9, October–December 1983.

6. Eduardo Aunós, "La emoción de la fotografía," in *Álbum Fotográfico Luz y Sombras*, Madrid, 1948.

7. Quoted by Manuel Sendón and X. Luis Suárez Canal in the catalog of the exhibition *En Galiza nos 50. As agrupacións fotográficas*, Concello de Vigo, 1990.

8. Luis Alonso Tejada, "La represión sexual en la España de Franco," in *Historia-16*, Madrid, February 1977.

THE DAWN OF REALITY

9. Alexandre Cirici. Conference held in April 1958 and reported in the magazine *Afal*, number 25, July–August 1960.
Brassaï, "Images latentes," in *L'Intransigeant*, Paris, 15 November 1932.

10. Antonio Muñoz Molina, text from Ricardo Martín, *Sostener la mirada*, Junta de Andalucía, Granada, 1993.

11. Alexandre Cirici, "Monocle, bisturi i Luna Park," in the newspaper *Avui*, Barcelona, 28 March 1982.

THROUGH FOREIGN EYES

12. Neither Spain nor any Spanish photographers were represented in this exhibition, which, paradoxically, exerted so much influence on the renewal of Spanish photography in the 1950s and 1960s. Two single images, taken by Robert Frank and Leonti Plankoy, made up the flimsy "Spanish" presence in this monumental show, which toured dozens of countries and drew millions of people.

13. In fact, Smith was well aware of the importance of reportage, even from the moment he was commissioned by *Life*. "I am about to embark," he wrote to Carmen Smith Wood on 10 March 1950, "on one of the most important pieces of work that I will ever do. It involves my living in a small Spanish village and working in the middle of the poverty and fear of Franco's Spain. I hope that this will be the strongest and most moving photographic essay of my life, in that the theme offers a great deal of scope, as much from the viewpoint of a magazine reportage as from a human or artistic point of view."

(Letter quoted by Jim Hughes in *W. Eugene Smith, Shadow and Substance—The Life and Work of an American Photographer*), 1989.

14. Jean Dieuzaide, "Por qué España." Published in the catalog of the exhibition *Jean Dieuzaide*, Sala Parpalló, Valencia, 1990. Contributors to the catalog include Gilles Mora, Florence Guillaume, and Mateo Gamón.

15. A selection of Inge Morath's "Spanish" photographs were shown in *Inge Morath, España, años 50*, an exhibition organized by Lola Garrido in 1994, with an excellent catalog.

ENFORCING THE DICTATORSHIP

16. "Very often goods were exchanged for the cameras that sailors brought back in their boats. In Barcelona, prostitutes whose clients included sailors gave their services in exchange for cameras, which they then resold to local tradesmen." Gerardo Acereda Valdés, in a letter to the author, 29 January 1994.

17. "This company was by far the biggest in the national market and between 1980 and 1986 it exported 400,000 items to 40 different countries, among which, curiously enough, numbered Japan, which received 15,000 items." Gerardo Acereda Valdés, "Cámaras fotográficas españolas," in the magazine *FV*, issue 64, Madrid, 1993. By 1986, Cerlex was exporting 55,000 cameras a year, according to figures supplied by the magazine *Foto Profesional* (Madrid, January 1986).

18. Figures published in the magazine *Cambio-16*, 13 July 1981.

19. From an article published in the bulletin *Ecos Negra*, number 28, 1968, in which it is stated that in 1967, 2,000 people were employed in the Spanish photographic industry.

20. José Aumente, in the bulletin of the *Sindicato Nacional del Papel y Artes Gráficas*, number 6, Madrid, November–December 1972.

21. Manuel López Rodríguez, "La fotografía: una realidad desenfocada," in *Foto Profesional*, number 24, Madrid, October 1985.

22. Joan Fontcuberta, in an interview with Josep Rigol, in *Camera Internacional*, Spanish edition, May–June 1988.
Xavier Miserachs, *Profesiones con futuro. Fotógrafo*, Grijalbo-Mondadori, Barcelona, 1995.

23. This issue was still exercising Jorge Rueda in 1991. "The first piece of flippancy that I allow myself to astonish you with is that photography has nothing to do with art. At least, if I stick to what is strictly photography. That it was reputedly invented as something that can be reproduced and the main reason that it has prospered is that it can be reproduced as an original work, though the moment this happens it loses its uniqueness. That it cannot be reproduced nor copied. I say that what a photograph holds is quite independent of the paper it is printed on, so that, being self-perpetuation, it can be repeated as many times as required, losing its character as a unique piece but without losing an atom of its primary and creative originality." Jorge Rueda, "De lejos y de cerca. Fotografía española contemporánea," in *El Paseante*, number 18–19, Madrid, 1991.

24. Quoted by Xosé Luis Suárez Canal and Manuel Sendón, *op. cit.* Vigo, 1992. "Anything that did not have a strictly photographic, and one might almost say a strictly technical, purpose was forbidden. The nude in photographic or social denunciation, for example, could present problems for these bodies." Carlos Cánovas, *Apuntes para una historia de la fotografía en Navarra*, Gobierno de Navarra, Pamplona, 1992.

25. "The premises of the Sociedad Fotográfica de Zaragoza in 1983 was a space at street level measuring little more than 100 square yards all told. As you entered, you came to a small lobby curtained off from the main room; this tiny space, with barely room enough for a table, was the office. The laboratory, shabby and full of bottles of chemicals, was equipped only with a Durst, a Carranza, and an old laminating machine. I was deeply disappointed to discover that the society that I had so idealized was such a modest place." Vicente Blasco, "Mis impresiones y la evolución de la Sociedad Fotográfica de Zaragoza en los últimos 10 años," Sociedad Fotográfica de Zaragoza bulletin, Zaragoza, May–June 1983.

26. Steinert's work made such a stir in Spain that *Afal* was obliged to justify its overdue exhibition: "As in other areas of photography and of the spirit, these last few years, and for reasons beyond its control, Spain has had its back turned to intellectual developments in Europe. It is still appropriate now, in 1961, to be looking at what for the rest of Europe ten years ago was the greatest artistic innovation." Catalog to the retrospective exhibition *Otto Steinert, 1950–1960, Afal* magazine, Almería, 1961.

27. "The magazine is a very clear example of the feeble results that normally come from outdated or hidebound attitudes. Nothing new can come out of old attitudes." Carlos Serrano, observations on *Cuadernos de Fotografía*, in *Nueva Lente*, number 12, Madrid, February 1973.

28. Xavier Miserachs, "El Trofeo Luis Navarro," in *Imagen y Sonido*, number 13, Barcelona, January 1965. "Guidelines provided by the small enclosed world of exhibitions became established as a kind of internal logic impervious to any outside influences; by the very fact that they were alien to the peculiar milieu of competitions, these guidelines were without value." Enric Mira, *La vanguardia fotográfica de los años setenta en España*, Instituto de Cultura Juan Gil-Albert, Alicante, 1991.

29. Oriol Maspons, "Salonismo," in *Arte Fotográfico*, number 61, Madrid, January 1957.

30. The prize money of the Premio Negtor, awarded every other year since 1958, was 54,000 pesetas ($360) in 1960. That year, 915 photographers submitted 2,271 works. In 1966 the prize money had risen to 99,000 pesetas ($660). In 1970, the Premio Negtor underwent radical change: photographs that were submitted now had to have won prizes in competitions organized by the 50 societies that supported the prize. Through 42 competitions, almost 200 works were selected, the winner being awarded 100,000 pesetas ($670). (Figures provided by Rosario Martínez Rochina, published in the newsletter *Ecos Negra*.)

31. Traveling photographers have been described by the writer Julio Llamazares: "He turned up one morning at the school, camera and tripod in hand, and his case slung from this shoulder. He was quite advanced in years, and was wearing a hat and a striped suit, and that strange look of men who wearily travel the world. He set up the tripod in the middle of the school, and one by one each of us sat at the headmaster's table, on which had been placed an exercise book and a pen, and the world globe that we used to keep in the cupboard. The backcloth was a folded sheet and the map that I helped him pin over the blackboard." Julio Llamazares, "Escenas de cine mudo," Seix-Barral, Barcelona, 1994.

32. According to Alfredo Romero, Jalón Ángel's productivity was topped only by the firm Amer-Ventosa, which, between 1957 and 1975 produced almost one million portraits. Alfredo Romero, "Jalón Ángel entre el pictorialismo y el retratismo profesional," in *Jalón Ángel*, Diputación Provincial de Zaragoza, Zaragoza, 1985.

33. Not everyone accepted this "resurrection" of the photographer. "One cannot, however much one might want to, shake off the memory," wrote an anonymous contributor to the daily newspaper *El Alcázar*. "A photographer, of royalty and the great figures of our society, would delight in spreading his work all over the sensationalist press … The fact that this photographer publicly flaunts his name, the advertisement for his studios, in a street in the center of town, gets on our nerves a little. Let him work, but work quietly, without drawing attention to himself, because he must not provoke those who remember." "Cuidado con la memoria," in *El Alcázar*, Madrid, July 30 1942.

34. *Nueva Lente*, November 1972.

35. "The absolute power of the photographer who focuses on the foreground to excess, so as to emphasize invisible details, or who includes in the shot an accumulation of symbolic objects … can also become irritating. Clearly, the most successful images are those that hold our attention before we can decipher the detail and there are so many successful images that some of the more pompous ones can end up making the viewer feel uncomfortable." Christian Caujolle, "De la realidad del retrato," in the catalog to the exhibition *Alberto Schommer Retratos, 1969–1989*, Lunwerg Editores, Barcelona–Madrid, 1989.

36. The press of the Nationalist Movement took its inspiration in fair measure from the experience of the Nazi propaganda department. According to Román Gubern, Germany controlled a few publishing houses, such as *Sofindas* and *Hisma*; daily newspapers, such as *Informaciones*; broadcasters, such as Radio Valladolid; and exhibition halls and movie distributors. Román Gubern, *La Censura. Función y ordenamiento jurídico bajo el franquismo*, Península, Barcelona, 1981.

37. Authorities like Fernández Areal maintain that the system of censorship and control remained in force until some years after the Fraga Law was passed in April 1966. Manuel Fernández Areal, *La libertad de prensa en España*, Cuadernos para el Diálogo, Madrid, 1971.

38. José Nuñez Larraz, *Seis décadas de fotografía*, Junta de Castilla y León, Salamanca, 1993.

39. Despite his known links with freemasonry, Campúa junior was for many years General Franco's sole photographer. "Carmen, my daughter, reproached me for keeping Campúa as El Pardo's only photographer. That Campúa was known as a freemason is beyond doubt, but whatever you expect me to say, I like his photographs and when I see myself in a photograph not taken by Campúa I look like someone that I am not." Manuel Vázquez Montalbán, *Autobiografía del general Franco*, Planeta, Barcelona, 1992.

40. Jaume Fabre, *Història del fotoperiodisme a Catalunya, 1885–1976*, Col·legi de Periodistes de Catalunya, Barcelona, 1990. Josep Cruañas i Tor, various articles published in the magazine *Capçalera* between 1989 and 1991.

41. Enrique Bustamante, *Los amos de la información*, Akal, Madrid, 1982. For information on agencies see Diego Caballo Ardila, *El editor gráfico de prensa en las agencias con redes mundiales de telegrafía*, doctoral thesis, February 1995.

42. Xavier Miserachs, *op. cit.*, Barcelona, 1995.

43. Manuel López Rodríguez, "Fotógrafos, ergo periodistas," in *Nueva Lente*, number 107–108, July–August 1981.

44. Juan Luis Cebrián, *La prensa y la calle*, Nuestra Cultura, Madrid, 1980.

45. The fate of the photographs taken by Manel Armengol during a peaceful demonstration organized by the Asamblea de Cataluña on 1 February 1976 illustrates the climate of repression that prevailed at the time. Such photographs were illegal and had to be smuggled out of Spain, to appear in various European and US publications.

46. During those years, various picture agencies were established, although none survived for long. They included *Delta Press, Seite Press,* and *Blasón*—the redoubt of the enlightened, in the words of Guillermo Armengol, one of the founders of *Blasón*—but all three were commercial failures. Other agencies that emerged during the years of transition to democracy were *Pull*, of which Antonio Suárez was a cofounder, and *Copi,* established by Juan Santiso and Joaquín Amestoy. *Cosmo Press*, different from the others, was founded by César Lucas and Setimio Garritano in 1965. *Cover's* great innovation, apart from the excellent quality of its material, was the creation of a solid commercial infrastructure, which allowed it to face the future with a certain degree of optimism.

47. According to Salustiano del Campo, in 1970 fewer than 3,360,000 Spanish workers, out of a total of 12,854,500 economically active people, were living outside Spain. Salustiano del Campo, *Análisis de la población española*, Guadiana, Madrid, 1972.

48. Manuel Vázquez Montalbán, *La penetración americana en España*, Cuadernos para el Diálogo, Madrid, 1974.

49. Juan Goytisolo, *El furgón de la cola*, Seix-Barral, Barcelona, 1976.

50. José María Artero, "Nuestra postura," in *Afal*, number 4, Almería, July 1958. "The rivalry," wrote Brassaï in 1932, "was not between painting and photography but between photographic painting and painterly photography. Let them destroy each other, kill each other, so that we may be rid of them forever!" Brassaï: "Images latentes," in *L'Intransigeant*, Paris, 15 November 1932.

51. Xavier Miserachs, *op. cit.*, Barcelona, 1995.

52. Luis Conde Vélez, "Lo nuevo en fotografía," in *Arte Fotográfico*, Madrid, February 1953.

53. Gabriel Cualladó, "Cómo hago mis fotografías," in *Arte Fotográfico*, number 69, Madrid, September 1957. Gonzalo Juanes, "Cómo hago mis fotografías," in *Arte Fotográfico*, number 66, Madrid, June 1957.

54. José María Artero, "La revista AFAL y aquellos locos fotógrafos de los 50–60," in the catalog of the exhibition *Grupo AFAL, 1956–1991*, Almería, 1991.

55. Arcilaga, "La realidad desnuda no es tema de arte," in *Arte Fotográfico*, number 96, Madrid, January 1969.

AFAL'S REVOLUTION

56. Xavier Miserachs, in a letter to the author, May 1995.

57. André Thevenez, *Photo-Revue*, November 1956.

58. Gabriel Cualladó, in conversation with the author, spring 1994.

59. "The realist photography that became established in Spain from the mid-1950s has failed because photographers have not had sufficient courage to face the country's burning issues, merely focusing instead on the external, monotonous landscape of what passes for real life." Elías Dolcet, "Comentario a la fotografía *El empalao*, de Juan Dolcet," in the bulletin of the Real Sociedad Fotográfica de Madrid, May 1973.

60. "Cualladó was never committed to contemporary history in the way that Smith was. He was too unique, too much an individualist to endorse the concept of the people, including the 'populism' on which neorealism is based …. Compared with Smith's humanitarian approach, his work has developed in a minor key, restricted to the world of vernacular culture." Jean-François Chevrier, "La mirada humanista," in the catalog of the exhibition *Gabriel Cualladó. Fotografías*, Valencia, 1989.

61. Carlos Pérez Siquier, in conversation with the author, summer 1994.

62. The important presence of photographers of the Barcelona group contrasts with the almost complete absence of the nucleus of the Madrid group, whose participation was limited to some photographs by Vielba and, especially, by Cualladó and Paco Gómez. In fact, in *Afal's* retrospective exhibition, only the latter two figure among those whose work was selected, together with Miserachs, Masats, Maspons, Ontañón, Terré, Schommer, and Pérez Siquier.

63. "These societies had variously embraced realism, tailoring it to fit the requirements of the exhibition-salon, juggled with a few informalist ideas of whose origin they had no idea and firmly stuck to the same technical assumptions as always." Carlos Cánovas, "Entre dos rupturas," in the catalog of the exhibition *Tiempo de silencio*, Barcelona, 1992.

64. "For us," affirmed J. M. Casademont, "photography was a problem of living by our chosen profession. What we really wanted was to become professional photographers. The fact that our endeavor was to have a merit all of its own, which we achieved not by escaping up the path of surrealism, for example, but through social criticism, I believe is completely accidental." "Fotografía catalana. Entre la documentació i l'estètica," a conversation between Josep María Casademont and Joan Fontcuberta, in *Serra D'Or*, Barcelona, December 1982.

THE BIRTH OF THE FUTURE

65. Restrictions on freedom of the press took the form of a stepping up of disciplinary action against newspapers and magazines, including *Triunfo, Destino, Madrid, Sábado Gráfico,* and *Cuadernos para el Diálogo*. The defining case was that of the newspaper *Madrid*, which was ordered to close down in 1971, as a clear warning to those sectors of the press that took a hostile stand against the regime.

66. Valeriano Bozal, *Arte del siglo XX en España*, volume II, Espasa-Calpe, Madrid, 1995.

67. Javier Herrera, "Rafael Canogar," in *Nueva Lente*, Madrid, May 1982. Javier Herrera produced a documentary series on the relationship between painting and photography, which was published in successive issues of *Nueva Lente*, and a special issue of July–August 1982.

68. Eduardo Subirats, *Después de la lluvia*, Temas de Hoy, Madrid, 1994.

69. It should not be forgotten that those young photographers who were associated with *Nueva Lente* were squarely opposed to the critical realism of such artists as Genovés, Canogar, the *Crónica*, and Antonio Saura himself, against whom they brandished the true rage of a younger generation. This stance, adopted by Rafael and Luis Pérez Mínguez, came to the fore in the Sala *Amadís,* whose director was Juan Antonio Aguirre, the creator and leader of the so-called *New Generation*. Enric Mira, who has carried out a detailed study of the *Nueva Lente* phenomenon, has pointed out the importance of the *New Generation* in the genesis of the magazine. Enric Mira, "La ubicuidad de Nueva Lente en la diversidad estética de la España de los setenta," at a conference published in the minutes of the Jornadas de Estudio *Nueva Lente*, which took place in Madrid in October 1993.

70. Enric Mira: *op. cit*. Pere Formiguera, one of the most typical members of the *Nueva Lente* generation—which with absolutely no care for historical accuracy was termed the *Fifth Generation*—recently acknowledged this dubious neglect of the past: "We are looking back in anger without stopping to separate the wheat from the chaff; we are putting everything into the same basket and throwing the whole thing out. We did not realize, I admit, that that basket contained hidden treasure. It contained the efforts and achievements of *Afal* … and photographs by the *Madrid School* … Even today I ask myself what madness made one avant-garde group reject the other. What we were rejecting, they had rejected before us; what we were defending, they had already defended; and what we were criticizing they had denounced ad nauseam." Pere Formiguera, "De la quinta a la cuarta con un abrazo a destiempo," in the catalog of the exhibition *Fotógrafos de la Escuela de Madrid*, Madrid, 1988.

71. "Of the little that I know of Spanish photography," stated Colin Osman, editor of *Creative Camera*, "I find this tradition of surrealism surprising … an aggressive and violent kind of surrealism, devoid of content, that only seeks to shock the viewer. And this thing of 'épater la bourgeoisie,' in the vein of Picabia and Man Ray, was being done 70 years ago: photography should have moved on." Colin Osman, in an interview with Joan Fontcuberta, in *Nueva Lente*, number 62, April 1977.

72. Enric Mira identified three completely different phases in the life of *Nueva Lente*: the eclectic phase, under Pablo Pérez Mínguez and Carlos Serrano (1971–75); the surrealist phase, under Jorge Rueda (1975–78); and the amateur and competition phase, under Salvador Obiols. There was also a final phase, under the editorship of Matías Antolín, in which the importance of restoring and looking into photography became an issue, with contributions by Marie-Loup Sougez, Lee Fontanella, and Publio López Mondéjar.

73. Albert Guspi was a determining presence in the creation of a struggling, incipient market for photography. It was nurtured by the intermittent activities of his own gallery and that of others like *Redor*, in Madrid, founded in 1970 by Tino Calabuig; *Baltá*, which opened in Barcelona in 1972; *Parpalló*, established in Valencia in 1980; and *Forum* in Tarragona, set up by David Balcells and Chantal Grande, as well as the activities of other galleries that did not specialize in photography, like *Multitud, Maeght,* and *Fernando Vijande*. Most of these galleries met with commercial failure and it is telling that only three have managed to survive.

74. "Those photographers that cannot accept that they are not considered to be 'real artists' come out with a whole catalog of ruses to secure their understandable and, in their view, deserved cultural position. To do that they may paint, cut, turn, or manipulate their images so as to give them a wholesome appearance. For them, like the pictorialists before them, these titivated 'things' thus acquire originality and exclusivity (or, rather, inaccessibility). Consequently, when they come to sell their work, they become a 'famous artist'. It is a shame that, having taken so much trouble, this is of so little use to them." Pablo Pérez Mínguez, "La fotografía … ¿antiarte?" in *Nueva Lente*, number 25, Madrid, March 1974.

THE PHOTOGRAPHS

ANONYMOUS. Children saluting. 1939. (Efe Archive)

JUAN ANTONIO AVILÉS. Political prisoners with prison guards and officers at Huéscar prison. Granada, c. 1940. (Mercedes Avilés Collection)

JUAN ANTONIO AVILÉS. Funerals of "los Caídos" (the Fallen Ones), in Galera, Granada, 1939. (Mercedes Avilés Collection)

FEDERICO VÉLEZ. Members of the first Consistorio Municipal de Burgos, after the war. 1940. (Vélez Archive)

HERMES PATO. Spanish "producers" leave for Germany. Madrid, 25 November 1941. (Efe Archive)

JAUME CALAFELL. A women's basketball team. Tárrega, Lérida, 1942. (Calafell Archive, Tárrega)

ALEJANDRO MERLETTI. Authorities at an official gathering. Barcelona, 1943. (Institut d'Estudis Fotogràfics de Catalunya)

SANTOS YUBERO. The hairdressing salon at Porlier prison. Madrid, August 1941. (Archivo de la Comunidad de Madrid)

ANONYMOUS. Political prisoners in the old Puerto de Santa María prison. June 1948. (Efe Archive)

PEDRO MENCHÓN. The dining room at the social center. Lorca, Murcia, 1945. (Archivo Municipal de Lorca)

PEDRO MENCHÓN. An old people's home. Lorca, c. 1945. (Archivo Municipal de Lorca)

SANTOS YUBERO. Crowds wave goodbye to the Blue Division at the Estación del Norte. Madrid, June 1941. (Santos Yubero Archive, Comunidad de Madrid)

SANTOS YUBERO. Aurora Berja wearing the Cruz de Hierro (Iron Cross) awarded to her son Nemesio García, a member of the Blue Division, who died on the Soviet front. Madrid, May 1942. (Comunidad de Madrid)

ALEJANDRO MERLETTI. Holy mission. Barcelona, 1945. (Institut d'Estudis Fotogràfics de Catalunya)

HERMENEGILDO VALLVÉ. A prisoner's wife tries to give General Franco a letter. Tarragona, 1949. (Foto-Cine Vallvé)

ORTIZ ECHAGÜE. A religious procession in Turégano. 1947. (Legado Ortiz Echagüe, University of Navarre)

ORTIZ ECHAGÜE. A Castilian shepherd. c. 1955. (Legado Ortiz Echagüe, University of Navarre)

ANTONI CAMPAÑÁ. *Harvest*. Bromóleo. 1942. (Campañá Family Collection)

CARLOS GUTIÉRREZ. *Pastoral*. 1947. (Carlos Gutiérrez Collection)

EDUARDO SUSANNA. Shepherd. 1948. (Real Sociedad Fotográfica)

PLÁ JANINI. *The last prayer*. Bromóleo. 1940s. (Plá i Guarro Collection)

PLÁ JANINI. *Under the arches*. Bromóleo. 1946. (Plá i Guarro Collection)

EUGENE SMITH. Spinner, from *The Spanish Village*. Deleitosa, May 1950. (Cualladó Collection, Instituto Valenciano de Arte Moderno)

EUGENE SMITH. Three Guardia Civil officers, from *The Spanish Village*. Deleitosa, 22 May 1950. (Magnum-Zardoya)

JEAN DIEUZAIDE. Street market. Lorca, 1951. (Photographer's collection)

JEAN DIEUZAIDE. Gypsy woman from El Sacromonte. Granada, 1951. (Photographer's collection)

MICHAEL WOLGENSINGER. Herd of pigs on the banks of the Tormes river. Salamanca, 1953. (Wolgensinger Archive)

MICHAEL WOLGENSINGER. Roadbuilding. Andalusia, 1953. (Wolgensinger Archive)

MARC RIBOUD. Toledo, 1959. (Riboud Archive)

INGE MORATH. Seminarians in Plaza del Callao. Madrid, 1953. (Inge Morath-Magnum)

MARC RIBOUD. Official
opening
of the Valle de los Caídos.
1 April 1949. (Riboud Archive)

AMER-VENTOSA. Untitled. 1950s. (Ana Muller Collection)

AMER-VENTOSA. Carmencita Franco in a wedding dress. 1950. (Ana Muller Coll.)   AMER-VENTOSA. Admiral Carrero Blanco. c. 1955. (Ana Muller Coll.)

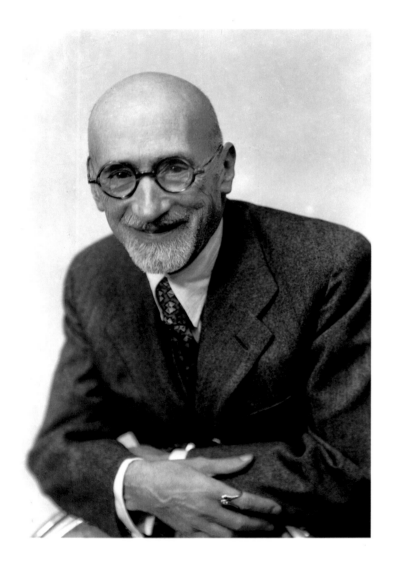 

LEOPOLDO CARTAGENA. Jacinto Benavente. 1941. (Cartagena Archive)

M. DUART. Dr Fleming. c. 1950. (Institut d'Estudis Fotogràfics de Catalunya)

PEDRO MARÍA IRURZUN. Señor Toldrá. 1950. (Lidia Anoz Collection)

ALFONSO SÁNCHEZ PORTELA. José Martínez Ruiz *Azorín*. 1948. (Private collection)

NICOLÁS MULLER. Pío Baroja walking in Buen Retiro park. Madrid, 1950. (Muller Archive)

JUAN GYENES. Lola Flores. c. 1950. (Gyenes Archive)   JUAN GYENES. Sara Montiel. 1945. (Gyenes Archive)

PÉREZ DE LEÓN. The cabaret artist Gogó Rojo. c. 1968. (Pérez de León Archive)

VICENTE IBÁÑEZ. Manuel Benítez, *El Cordobés.* 1964. (Ibáñez Archive)

VICENTE IBÁÑEZ. The dancer Antonio. 1963. (Ibáñez Archive)

VICENTE IBÁÑEZ. Tere del Río. 1953. (Ibáñez Archive)

ALBERTO SCHOMMER. *A cardinal trying to sort out the confusion.* Cardinal Tarancón. 1969. (Círculo de Bellas Artes de Madrid)

ALBERTO SCHOMMER. *Grasping space.* Eduardo Chillida. 1972. (Photographer's collection)

ORIOL MASPONS. *Jeanette the bee-hunter.* 1967. (Photographer's collection)

LEOPOLDO POMÉS. Elsa. 1962. (Photographer's collection)

LEOPOLDO POMÉS. Julio Cortázar. 1967. (Photographer's collection)

LEOPOLDO POMÉS. Óscar Tusquets. 1974. (Photographer's collection)

TONI VIDAL. Joan Fuster. 1972. (Photographer's collection)

JUAN DOLCET. Manolo Millares. 1960. (Dolcet Family)

ÁNGEL ESTEBAN. Arrest of Eleuterio Sánchez, *El Lute*, on the Valdunciel road, Salamanca, 14 June 1966. (Efe Archive)

SANTIAGO ARINA. Official announcement of the Holy Mission. Vitoria, 1962. (Archivo Municipal de Vitoria)

ARQUE (F. Arocena and G. Querejazu). Monsignor Antoniutti, the papal nuncio, is greeted by Colonel Arciniega. Vitoria, April 1956. (Archivo Municipal de Vitoria)

A. MARTÍ VILLARDEFRANCOS. Emigrant children having missed the boat. Port of La Coruña, 1960. (Photographer's collection)

CARLOS PÉREZ DE ROZAS. Prisoners of the Blue Division arrive aboard the *Semiramis*. Barcelona, 3 April 1954. (Efe Archive)

MANUEL FERROL. An emigrant at confession before embarking for the United States. La Coruña, 1956. (Photographer's collection)
MANUEL FERROL. Emigrants' farewell. La Coruña, 1956. (Photographer's collection)

NICOLÁS MULLER. Little girls joining hands in a circle. Argamasilla de Alba, 1960. (Photographer's collection)

NICOLÁS MULLER. Listening to the governor. Argamasilla de Alba, 1960. (Photographer's collection)

JOSÉ SUÁREZ. Greeting the shrine of the Baby Jesus. La Mancha, 1965. (Suárez Family Collection)

JOSÉ SUÁREZ. A peasant setting off in search of work. La Mancha, 1965. (Suárez Family Collection)

CATALÁ ROCA. Young women walking along Gran Vía. Madrid, 1953. (Collection of the heirs of Catalá Roca)

CATALÁ ROCA. The proposition. Seville, 1959. (Collection of the heirs of Catalá Roca)

CATALÁ ROCA. *A hawker in Gerona market.* 1953. (Collection of the heirs of Catalá Roca)

CATALÁ ROCA. *Advertising.* Barcelona, 1957. (Collection of the heirs of Catalá Roca)

RAMÓN MASATS. Castilian peasants, from *Viejas historias de Castilla la Vieja*. 1964. (Photographer's collection)

RAMÓN MASATS. Tomelloso, 1960. (Photographer's collection)

RAMÓN MASATS. Madrid, 1957. (Photographer's collection)

RAMÓN MASATS. Madrid, 1961, from *Neutral Corner*. (Photographer's collection)

JOAN COLOM. Barcelona, 1959, from *Izas, rabizas y colipoterras.* (Photographer's collection)

JOAN COLOM. Barcelona, 1959, from *Izas, rabizas y colipoterras.* (Photographer's collection)

CARLOS PÉREZ SIQUIER. La Chanca, Almería. 1962. (Photographer's collection)

◁ CARLOS PÉREZ SIQUIER. Tabernas, Almería. 1962. (Photographer's collection)

CARLOS PÉREZ SIQUIER. Twins on public display at the fair. Almería, 1973. (Photographer's collection)

LEOPOLDO POMÉS. At an amateur bullfight in La Algaba, Seville. 1957. (Photographer's collection)

FRANCISCO ONTAÑÓN. Wedding in Salamanca. 1960. (Photographer's collection)

FRANCISCO ONTAÑÓN. Andalusian family. 1960. (Photographer's collection)

GERARDO VIELBA. El Sardinero beach. Santander, 1960. (Photographer's collection)

GERARDO VIELBA. A stroll along the quay. Santander, 1973. (Photographer's collection)

XAVIER MISERACHS. Carrer d'Escudellers. Barcelona, 1962. (Photographer's collection)

XAVIER MISERACHS. El Born market. Barcelona, 1962. (Photographer's collection)

XAVIER MISERACHS. Immigrants leaving Francia station. Barcelona, 1962 (Photographer's collection)

XAVIER MISERACHS. A proposition in Vía Layetana. Barcelona, 1962. (Miserachs Collection)

RICARD TERRÉ.
Holy Week.
Vigo, 1957.
(Photographer's
collection)

RICARD TERRÉ.
Holy Week.
Sant Boi de
Llobregat, 1957.
(Photographer's
collection)

ORIOL MASPONS. Group of gypsies. La Mancha, 1960. (Photographer's collection)

ORIOL MASPONS. Bullfight in a La Mancha village. 1961. (Photographer's collection)

FRANCISCO GÓMEZ. *The candle-seller of Atocha Street.* Madrid, 1966. (Photographer's collection)

FRANCISCO GÓMEZ. Family portrait. Turégano, Segovia, 1969. (Photographer's collection)

FRANCISCO GÓMEZ. A factory worker at Plata Meneses. Madrid, 1971. (Photographer's collection)

FRANCISCO GÓMEZ. Woman at prayer. 1973. (Photographer's collection)

GABRIEL CUALLADÓ. Secretary at Alarcón town hall. Cuenca, 1968. (Photographer's collection)

GABRIEL CUALLADÓ. The waiting room,
Atocha Station. Madrid, 1957.
(Photographer's collection)

GABRIEL CUALLADÓ. Organ-grinder on Toledo Bridge. Madrid, 1960. (Photographer's collection)

GABRIEL CUALLADÓ. Miner. La Folguera, 1958. (Photographer's collection)

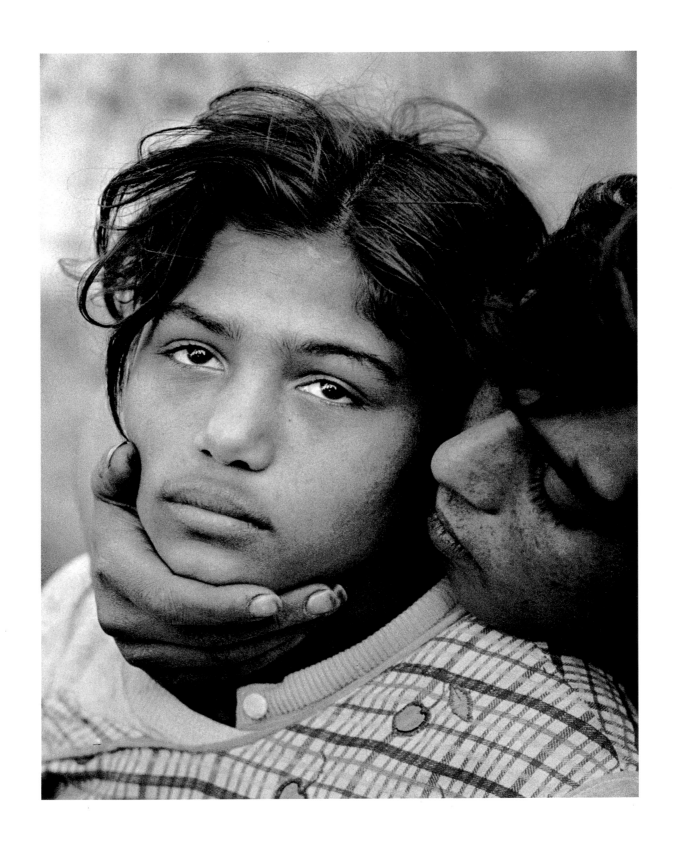

EUGENIO FORCANO. *The Look.* Children from the slums of Montjuïc. Barcelona, 1964. (Photographer's collection)
EUGENIO FORCANO. Delivery man in Ciutat Vella. Barcelona, 1964. (Photographer's collection)

JUAN DOLCET. Living effigy for Holy Week. Valverde de la Vera, 1968. (Dolcet Family Collection)

FERNANDO GORDILLO. Bakers of Pedro Bernardo. 1967. (Photographer's collection)

FERNANDO GORDILLO. Vigil in Pedro Bernardo. 1969. (Photographer's collection)

JORDI OLIVÉ. *The dead baby girl.* Alforja, Tarragona, 1965. (Societat Fotográfica de Reus. Obra Cultural Caixa de Tarragona.)

RAFAEL SANZ LOBATO. Procession in Bercianos de Aliste. 1971. (Photographer's collection)

RAFAEL SANZ LOBATO. Miranda del Castañar. 1971. (Photographer's collection)

ÁNGEL QUINTAS. The fairground. Zamora, 1960. (Quintas Collection, Filmoteca de Castilla-León)

ÁNGEL QUINTAS. Plaza de la Constitución. Zamora, c. 1960. (Quintas Collection, Filmoteca de Castilla-León)

ANTONIO GABRIEL. Procession at Nosa Señora do Corpiño. Pontevedra province, 1963. (Collection of the photographer's family)

CÉSAR LUCAS. Luis Miguel Dominguín and El Cordobés out shooting. Toledo mountains, 1968. (Photographer's collection)

CRISTÓBAL HARA. Castilla la Mancha. 1969. (Photographer's collection)

TONI CATANY. Ibiza. 1967. (Photographer's collection)

RAMÓN ZABALZA.
From *Gitanos* (Gypsies).
Vicálvaro, 1975.
(Photographer's collection)

STINA GARCÍA RODERO.
The confession.
Saavedra, 1978.
Photographer's collection)

KOLDO CHAMORRO. Sanfermines. Pamplona, 1977. (Photographer's collection)

FERNANDO HERRÁENZ. La Mancha, 1971. (Photographer's collection)

CARLOS CORCHO. Holy Week. Madrid, 1970. (Photographer's collection)

JORGE RUEDA.
Plaza de Oriente. 1971.
(Photographer's collection)

GERMÁN GALLEGO. Political repression. Vitoria, March 1976. (Photographer's collection)

JORDI SOCIAS.
By the rules.
Barcelona, 1976.

AURORA FIERRO. General Franco's funeral. 1975. (Cover Archive)

FÉLIX LORRIO. Celebrations of 2 May. Madrid, 1977. (Photographer's collection)

THE PHOTOGRAPHERS

ALGUERSUARI, FRANCESC

Francesc Alguersuari Durán was born in Sabadell in 1919. He began his career as a photographer in 1942, at the same time as devoting himself to various sports. In 1942 his first photograph was published, in *Mundo Deportivo*, and this led to his working for various press media and for the photographic agency Efe. In 1961 he established DAF, the electronics firm, where he manufactured the first Spanish-made electronic flash. In 1955 he took part for the first time in the Vuelta Ciclista (cycle race) in Spain and for many years has covered all kinds of sporting events, especially cycle races in Spain, France, Italy, and Catalonia.

Alguersuari has been awarded major sports photography prizes, such as World Sport (1971). He is a longstanding freelance photographer and his work has appeared in a large number of sporting magazines. However, the Colegio de Periodistas de Cataluña would not accept him as a member until 1991. He was made a member of the Olympic Order by the International Olympic Committee and is an honorary member of ANIGP. He also holds the Médaille de Reconnaissance Tour de France, and the Medalla de Oro al Mérito Ciclista. He heads an important family of sporting photographers, consisting of himself and his sons Josep María and Jaume.

AVILÉS, JUAN ANTONIO

Juan Antonio Avilés Sánchez was born in Cartagena, Murcia, in 1886. He trained in the studio of the photographer Ángel Martínez, with whom he worked as a press and portrait photographer. For many years he worked as a traveling photographer in villages in southern Murcia and northern Granada.

In 1912 he established his own photographic studio in Baza, Granada, where he worked until 1935. That year he moved to Huéscar, Granada. Like the majority of popular photographers of his time, Avilés practised all forms of photography. He was also a contributor to various periodicals and magazines, including *El Ideal* of Granada, *Blanco y Negro*, and *ABC*.

Avilés always made use of large-format cameras. Not even after the war did he turn to medium-format or 35-mm cameras. Throughout the Spanish Civil War he kept his studio open, although his work was severely curtailed by the difficulties that he experienced in obtaining suitable photographic materials. In the immediate postwar years he produced photographs that are of major documentary value and historical interest.

He died in Huéscar in January 1945.

BOTÁN

Fernando Botán Mon, who launched the Botán dynasty, was born in Madrid in 1908. From an early age he showed an interest in photography and bullfighting, and this quickly led to his working for the specialist press. From 1955 this line of work was continued by his son, Fernando Botán Castillo (who was born in Madrid, in 1935). The Botáns became enormously popular in bullfighting circles, as they traveled all over Spain to the country's most important bullrings. Their photographs appeared in all the major periodicals and magazines of the time.

In 1964 they embarked on an important publishing program, which materialized in the form of such books as *4 toreros, 4 estilos* (Bienvenida, Ordoñez, Camino y Litri, 1964), two monographs on *El Cordobés* (1966), *La tragedia de la fiesta* (1966), and *Crónicas Taurinas Gráficas* (1968–78). Photographs by the Botáns were also published in various books and photographic yearbooks, which led to the award of major prizes, such as World Press Photo in 1972 and 1973.

Botán Castillo died in 1983, five years before his father, the founder of the Botán dynasty. Their legacy is a priceless archive of more than 2 million images. Today the Botán agency is run by Carmen Botán and Santiago Ojeda.

Self-portrait

Gordillo

Self-portrait

CALAFELL, JAUME

Jaume Calafell Pifarré was born in Sant Guim de Freixenet in 1917. He was a pilot during the Spanish Civil War, but in about 1938 he began to work for *El Diario de Burgos*. In 1940 he set up a photographic studio in Tárrega, and very soon afterward established another branch in Mollerusa. A notable exponent of popular photography in the years following the Civil War, Calafell worked as a press photographer on the daily newspaper *Nueva Tárrega*.

In about 1950, he began a new line as an inventor and small-scale manufacturer of photographic materials. He was also a true pioneer in the filming of cinematographic documentaries. He was a contributor to various newspapers and magazines such as *El Caso*, *La Vanguardia*, *Diario de Lérida*, *El Correo Catalán*, and *La Mañana*, and his photographs have appeared in various one-man shows, such as the famous exhibition in Tárrega in 1985 or at the Institut d'Estudis Fotogràfics de Catalunya in 1990.

His work has also been shown in various group exhibitions, such as *Historia del Fotoperiodisme a Catalunya* in 1990.

He died in Tárrega in June 1986.

CANTERO, LEONARDO

Leonardo Cantero was born in Bilbao in 1907. After studying architecture for several years, he set up as an amateur photographer, and in 1950 entered the Real Sociedad Fotográfica in Madrid. As a member of the group La Palangana, he has always been considered as belonging to the Madrid School. His work has been shown in various exhibitions, such as the third Bienal Internacional in Pescara (1960), the second Salón Internacional in Tarrasa (1963), Fotografía Actual Española (1963), and in the exhibition Fotógrafos de la Escuela de Madrid (1988).

His photographs have appeared in various magazines and yearbooks, such as *Arte Fotográfico*, *Imagen y Sonido*, the 1958 edition of the *Afal* yearbook, *Everfoto*, *Photo Year Book,* and *Cuadernos de Fotografía*, on whose editorial board he served. His work has been widely exhibited, and he has been awarded prizes in various competitions and exhibitions, including the Luis Navarro prize and II Certamen *Sonimag* (1965). He was also active as a panel judge and lecturer, and exerted a degree of influence on younger generations of amateur photographers in Madrid associated with the Real Sociedad de Fotográfica.

He died in Madrid in 1995.

CATALÁ-ROCA, FRANCESC

Francesc Catalá-Roca was born in Valls, Tarragona, in 1922, the son of the celebrated photographer Pere Catalá-Pic. From childhood he devoted himself to photography, working as an assistant in his father's studio. In the 1940s and 1950s he worked intensively for a variety of newspapers and magazines, including *La Vanguardia*, *Destino*, *Gaceta Ilustrada*, and *Revista*. He also published many books and guides, among them *Tauromaquia* (1962), *Cuenca* (1956), *Madrid* (1964), and *Barcelona* (1954). His work constitutes a sort of bridge between that of avant-garde photographers before the war and that of avant-garde documentary photographers of the 1940s and 1950s, exerting a profound influence on certain members of the younger generations of photographers of the period.

In 1983 he was awarded the Premio Nacional de Artes Plásticas, and in 1992 the Generalitat de Cataluña presented him with the Premi d'Arts Plastiques and the Cruz de Sant Jordi. A year later an exhibition of his work, *Personajes de los años cincuenta*, was mounted at the Biblioteca Nacional in Madrid. In 1989, Marti Rom and J. M. García Ferrer published *Catalá Roca*, a detailed account of his work. In 1994 he published his latest book, *Foto-grafías A-cromáticas*. He is currently working on a book of color photographs of New York.

I. Marroyo

Sanz Lobato

Paco Gómez

COLOM, JUAN

Juan Colom was born in Barcelona in 1921. He was by profession an accountant but turned to photography in 1957, training at the Agrupación Fotográfica y Cinematográfica. His work was widely exhibited between 1958 and 1960, and that year he co-founded a group of photographers called El Mussol. He had his first one-man show in 1961 and three years later published the book *Izas, rabizas y Colipoterras*, with text by Camilo José Cela. This first documentary monograph had a strong impact in photographic circles at the time.

Colom has exhibited in many different cities and venues, and selections of his work have appeared in such magazines as *Imagen y Sonido*, *Afal*, and *Arte Fotográfico*. His photographs have also been published in various catalogs and yearbooks, such as those issued by *Afal* (1958) and *Tiempo de Silencio* (1922).

For some years now Colom seems to have been forgotten, although he is still working on a series of photographs of the underworld of Barcelona's district 5, an area populated by prostitutes, drug addicts, beggars, and drunks.

Several years ago he decided to stop working in black and white, albeit for purely practical reasons.

CORCHO, CARLOS

Carlos Hernández Corcho was born in Madrid in 1929. He was taking his first photographs by about 1945 and in 1958 he entered the Real Sociedad Fotográfica in Madrid. In 1966 he was a co-founder of the group La Colmena. Although the harshness of his chosen subject was at odds with the over-refined esthetic of the photographic establishment, he was awarded a gold medal by the International Federation of Art Photographers in 1960.

That year he began to dedicate himself professionally to photography. In 1970 he went to Mexico, where he worked as a television stills photographer. On his return to Spain he joined the staff of the magazine *Guadiana*. In 1976 he compiled his famous photoreportage on the bloody events that took place in Montejurra. He also worked as a staff photographer for the magazine *Interviu*.

His photographs have appeared in such weekly publications as *Triunfo, Cuadernos para el Diálogo, Cambio-16, Paris-Match*, and *Newsweek*. He has had several one-man shows, and his work has been shown in several exhibitions, and been published in such yearbooks and specialist magazines as *Everfoto, Coteflash, Aquí Imagen, La fotografía* and *Arte Fotográfico*.

CUALLADÓ, GABRIEL

Gabriel Cualladó Candel was born in Masanasa, Valencia, in 1925. He began taking photographs in 1951 and in 1956 enrolled at the Real Sociedad Fotográfica in Madrid. A year later he joined the group Afal and in 1959 was a cofounder of the group La Palangana.

He is the winner of some of the most prestigious national and international prizes, and his photographs have appeared in a cosmopolitan selection of magazines, catalogs, and yearbooks. He has also taken part in a large number of exhibitions, such as those held at IVAM in Valencia (1989), the Museo Español de Arte Contemporáneo (1985), and the Museo Thyssen (1995).

He has published his work in various personal monographs, such as *Gabriel Cualladó, fotografías* (1985), *Gabriel Cualladó* (IVAM, 1989), and *Cualladó, puntos de vista* (1995). A selection from his photographic oeuvre was shown at IVAM in Valencia in 1993.

Of the Spanish photographers of his generation, Cualladó is the best known internationally. In 1993 he was voted the best European photographer by the National Museum of Photography, Film and Television, in Great Britain. He was also awarded the Premio Nacional de Fotografía in 1994.

Self-portrait

DOLCET, JUAN

Juan Dolcet was born in Madrid in 1914. He began taking photographs in about 1950, and enrolled at the Real Sociedad Fotográfica in Madrid in 1954. He worked as a professional photographer from 1955, and his work was shown in many exhibitions and one-man shows in such cities as Madrid, Barcelona, Bordeaux, Salzburg, Cologne, and Buenos Aires.

He was a distinguished member of the Madrid School, and his work, alongside that of other members of the School, was shown in several exhibitions during the Semana Internacional de Gualajara in 1985 and at the Museo Español de Arte Contemporáneo in 1988.

His photographs have appeared in leading Spanish and foreign photographic magazines, in such yearbooks as that issued by *Arte Fotográfico* and *Everfoto*, and in several histories of photography. He is noted as a portrait photographer, and his work placed him on a par with the highest-ranking Spanish artists and sculptors of his time. A selection of his portraits of artists was exhibited at the Centro Nacional de Arte Reina Sofía (1992) and published in the book *Juan Dolcet, retratos de artistas* (1992).

He died in Madrid in 1990.

FERROL, MANUEL

Manuel Ferrol Fernández was born in Cabo Villano, La Coruña, in 1923. Although from a very early age he was member of photographic clubs and societies in Vigo and La Coruña, he was never very closely associated with them.

In 1953, with the help of the photographer Juan Manuel Castuera, he set up his first studio in Ferrol, specializing in portraits of children. A few years later he settled permanently in La Coruña. His involvement in motion pictures began in 1956, when he started working as a stills photographer on various movies. That year he produced *Emigración*, his famous photo-reportage that was to have major repercussions some years later.

In 1958 he went to Germany to take a course in color photography at the Hamburg Photo-Schule, and in 1953 he began working for TVE (Televisión Española) and on the newsreel NO-DO (Noticiarios y Documentales).

His photographs have been published in several magazines, yearbooks, and catalogs, and exhibited in several group and one-man shows, such as *Open Spain* (1993), *Tiempo de silencio* (1992,) and *Europa después del diluvio* (1995).

A selection of his photographs on the theme of emigration was published by the Centro de Estudios Fotográficos de Vigo in 1986.

FORCANO, EUGENIO

Eugenio Forcano Andreu was born in Barcelona in 1926. He began taking part in competitions and exhibitions from 1959 and became one of the most celebrated photographers of his time. He started working as a professional photographer in 1960, when he joined the staff of the weekly *Destino*. In 1956, with his brother José he set up Forcano studios, which specialized in portrait photography, media images, and fashion and advertising work.

His photographs have appeared in leading Spanish and foreign magazines, including *Imagen y Sonido, Arte Fotográfico, Afal, Don, Graphis,* and *Gaceta Ilustrada*, as well as in such yearbooks and catalogs as *Coteflash* (1973 and 1974) and *Everfoto* (1973 and 1976). He has also published several books, including *Guía de Barcelona* (1964) and *Festa Major* (1969).

Forcano is a highly adaptable photographer, and his work is extremely varied. In recent years he has been experimenting with color photography, achieving significant results in the creative exploration of form and expression.

Juan Dolcet

GÁLVEZ, ANTONIO

Antonio Gálvez was born in Barcelona in 1928. From 1962 to 1992 he lived in Paris. In 1969 he began to work in film with Luis Buñuel and in 1970 began producing his series on Gaudí and the collection of portraits "Mis amigos los cabezones" (My pig-headed friends).

From 1971 to 1972 he collaborated on various films and in 1973 began work on *Esa falsa luz del día* (That false light of day), about madness and suicide. From 1976 to 1979 he worked on the series *Antonio Gálvez y la descomposición de los mitos* (Antonio Gálvez and the destruction of legends). In 1987 he produced a series on the theme of the Ten Commandments.

His work has been exhibited in many galleries in Spain and elsewhere in Europe, including the Avignon Festival (1968), the Palais de Chaillot in Paris (1971), the Espace Oscar Niemeyer in Le Havre (1983), the Museo Cantini in Marseilles (1989), the Alcázar de los Reyes Cristianos in Córdoba (1990), the Museo de Albacete (1991), the Museo de Arte Reina Sofía (1992), the Palacio de la Virreina in Barcelona (1994), and the Palacio de Sástago in Zaragoza (1994).

His photographs have also appeared in numerous publications, and his books include *Antonio Gálvez. Alegoría de Luis Buñuel* (Córdoba, 1989) and *Buñuel, una relación circular con Antonio Gálvez* (Barcelona, 1994).

GÓMEZ, FRANCISCO

Francisco Gómez Martínez was born in Pamplona in 1918. In 1957 he joined the group Afal, and two years later was a co-founder of the group La Palangana. He has exhibited on numerous occasions with Gabriel Cualladó, and has had a number of one-man shows at such venues as Els Quatre Gats in Barcelona (1984) and the gallery Forum in Tarragona (1987). His photographs have appeared in magazines, yearbooks, and catalogs such as *Arte Fotográfico, Imagen y Sonido, Afal, Photography Year Book, Everfoto,* and *Cuadernos de Fotografía.* Chosen by the Italian group La Gondola to exhibit at the Venice Biennale of 1962, he has won important prizes and been nominated for major awards, among them the Luis Navarro prize in 1959. He was chosen to represent Spain in France in 1978 at the Rencontres internationales de la photographie in Arles.

Paco Gómez is one of the most brilliant and refined photographers of his generation, and also one of the most unjustifiably forgotten. His work has had a profound influence on the younger generation of photographers. In 1995, the Fundació "La Caixa" organized a retrospective exhibition of his photographs, which were published in the book *Francisco Gómez, la emoción construída.*

GOMIS, JOAQUÍN

Joaquín Gomis Serdañons was born in Barcelona in 1902. From 1920 to 1928 he lived in England and the United States, during which time he formed a close association with such intellectuals and artists as Salvador Espriu, Joan Miró, and J. L. Sert. He lived in Paris during the Spanish Civil War, and afterward settled permanently in Barcelona, where he began a close artistic collaboration with Miró.

In 1943 he was a co-founder of Club 49, through which he met members of such avant-garde artistic groups as Dau al Set and El Paso. In 1950 he published *Sagrada Familia de Gaudí*, with text by Alexandre Cirici. In 1955 he traveled to various countries, taking a large number of photographs.

In 1972, together with J. L. Sert, R. Noguera, and Miró himself, he worked to set up the Fundación Miró.

In 1986 he showed a selection of his photographs in the exhibition *Joaquín Gomis, la poética de la modernitat,* and 1994 saw the publication of the book *Joaquín Gomis–Joan Miró. Fotografías, 1941–1981,* which reveals the great painter's intimate creative world.

Joaquín Gomis died in Barcelona in 1991.

Self-portrait

César Lucas

Self-portrait

GORDILLO, FERNANDO

Fernando Gordillo was born in Madrid in 1933. In 1964, after taking photography courses in Germany, Spain, and Switzerland, he concentrated on working as a professional photographer. In 1972 he established and edited the periodical *Cuadernos de Fotografía*. He has received many awards, among them the Dédalo prize (1962), the Premio de Honor Abeja de plata in Guadalajara (1965), the Fotografía Actual national prize (1968), and the Egara prize (1967).

His photographs have appeared in various magazines, yearbooks, and catalogs, including *Arte Fotográfico*, *Imagen y Sonido*, *Everfoto*, and *Cuadernos de Fotografía*. He has also exhibited in many group and one-man shows, such as Inter-Pres in Moscow (1966), Photo-europ in Switzerland (1967), and at the Real Sociedad Fotográfica in Madrid.

In 1988 he was invited to show his work in the exhibition *Fotógrafos de la Escuela de Madrid*. He worked on his famous photo-reportage *Pedro Bernardo: su ser y su circunstancia* between 1960 and 1970.

He now combines working as an industrial and publicity photographer with producing such personal photographic essays as *Un día feliz*, *La belleza fugitiva*, and *Retratos en el jardín*.

GYENES, JUAN

Juan Gyenes Remenyi was born in Kosposvar, Hungary, in 1912. He set up his own studio in Madrid in 1948, and this soon became a central meeting place for fashionable *madrileños* of the time. Gyenes also compiled several collections of photographs, including *España mística*, which celebrate Spain, its people, and its culture. Over many years he exhibited his photographs in various one-man shows, such as *España la bella y las bellezas de España* (1979), *Cien bellezas de España* (1969), and *Ballet español* (1953).

His photographs have also appeared in such magazines as *Arte Fotográfico* and *Sombras* and in many national and foreign publications. He has also produced several books, among them *Ballet español* (1953), *Don Juan y el teatro en España* (1955), *Tauromachie* (Paris, 1957), *Antonio, el bailarín de España* (1964), *Gyenes por Gyenes* (1983), *Embajadas de España* (1989), and *Picasso-mito-Dalí* (1991).

The catalog of *Gyenes, 50 años en España*, a retrospective exhibition of his work, was published in 1991.

For more than 30 years Gyenes also worked as a visual chronicler of the Madrid theater world, and in 1991 he succeeded Alfonso as a member of the Academia de Bellas Artes.

He died in Madrid in 1995.

IBÁÑEZ, VICENTE

Vicente Ibáñez was born in Linares, Jaén, in 1930. The son, grandson, and great-grandson of photographers, he decided at an early age to follow the same career path. After the death of his father in 1947, he took over the family studio in Calle Montera, Madrid, and in 1951 set up on his own in Gran Vía. Known as "photographer of the stars," Vicente Ibáñez was for many years one of the best known and most highly esteemed portrait photographers in Madrid.

His photographs have appeared in several magazines, yearbooks, and catalogs, and he has shown his work in many group exhibitions and one-man shows. A book of his photographs of bullfighting, in which he shows an ability subtly to capture color and movement, remains unpublished. In 1991, the Consejería de Cultura de la Comunidad de Madrid organized a retrospective of his work entitled *Vicente Ibáñez. Vida de un fotográfo*, which toured to several other cities.

After working for the weekly publication *Interviu* for several years, he now works in his own studio in Madrid, where he keeps a valuable collection of over 3,000 original photographic portraits.

Self-portrait

Carlos Saura

IRURZUN, PEDRO MARÍA

Pedro María Irurzun was born in Pamplona in 1902. Although he began taking photographs from an early age, he only took up photography systematically from 1940. He was instrumental in setting up the Agrupación Fotográfica y Cinematográfica of Navarre in 1955. He contributed to such magazines as *Sombras* and *Arte Fotográfico*, and to the 1958 yearbook issued by *Luz y Sombras*.

In the early 1950s Irurzun worked on and off as an advertising photographer, and took part in various competitions and exhibitions, as the result of which he won many awards. His primary specialty, however, was portrait photography in which, as Carlos Cánovas has written, he combines "formal beauty and the devoted admiration of his subject with an impeccable studio technique."

His photographs have been shown and published in various group exhibitions and catalogs, such as *Apuntes para una historia de la fotografía en Navarra* (1989) by Carlos Cánovas, and *Tiempo de silencio* (1992).

He died in Pamplona in 1958.

JUANES, GONZALO

Gonzalo Juanes Cifuentes was born in Gijón in 1923. In 1950 he moved to Madrid, where he lived for about four years. During this time he was loosely associated with members of the Real Sociedad Fotográfica. In Paris in 1954 he met Oriol Maspons; the two men shared a similar outlook on the photographic establishment of the period, which they rejected.

In 1957 he returned to Gijón, from where he worked closely with the group Afal, whose bulletin soon became one of the most thorough, informed, and penetrating critical and news forums. In about 1965, creative exhaustion and the need to explore new mediums of expression led him to give up photography.

His articles and photographs have appeared in various magazines and yearbooks, including *Afal* and *Arte Fotográfico*. In 1990, he returned to black and white photography, having destroyed the negatives of the photographs he had taken between 1947 and 1962, his most creative period.

In 1994 he exhibited his latest photographs in the Palacio de Revillagigedo in Gijón.

LUCAS, CÉSAR

César Lucas was born in Cantiveros, Ávila, in 1941. He started working as a press photographer for the agency Europa Press in 1958. A year later he joined the staff of the daily newspaper *Pueblo*, remaining until 1965, when he established the agency Cosmo Press.

In 1973 he became the picture editor of the magazine *Gentleman* and, after a period on the staff of *Boccacio* and *Viajar*, he became one of the founders of the daily newspaper *El País*, on which he worked as picture editor.

In 1978, after a brief period as executive director of the Spanish edition of the magazine *Photo* (1976), Grupo Z invited him to become picture editor on the weekly magazine *Interviu*, where he began his famous nude studies of the most popular Spanish actresses of the time.

After working as editor-in-chief of the magazine *Panorama*, he became director of photography of Ediciones Reunidas, compiled from various business publications.

César Lucas has enjoyed a wide-ranging career, showing equal skill and dedication as portrait photographer, nude photographer, press photographer, advertising photographer, and fashion photographer.

Gualladó

LLOYD, OTHO

Otho St. Clair Lloyd was born in London in 1885. After periods of time in Geneva, Munich, Rome, Florence, and Paris, he decided to settle in Barcelona in 1916. Together with his wife, the painter Olga Sacharoff, he soon joined the city's artistic circles. Already profoundly interested in painting, Otho Lloyd quickly developed a strong interest in photography.

After the Spanish Civil War his interest in photography developed further and in 1940 he joined the Agrupación Fotográfica de Cataluña. His work does not exhibit the painterliness characteristic of the neopictorialism that exerted such a strong influence on members of Agrupación Fotográfica de Cataluña, although it never went beyond a certain formal academism.

Most of his photographs—around 1,000 original prints—now form part of a private collection in Barcelona. A selection of these photographs was exhibited by the Fundación La Caixa in 1992, when the catalog *Otho Lloyd* was also published.

MASATS, RAMÓN

Ramón Masats Tortera was born in Caldas de Montbuy, Barcelona, in 1931. He founded the group La Palangana. His work has appeared in many one-man shows and group exhibitions, and in most of the specialist publications.

His published books include *Neutral Corner* (1962), *Los Sanfermines* (1963), *Viejas Historias de Castilla la Vieja* (1964), *España diversa* (1984), *Andalucía* (1988), *Del cielo a España* (1989), and *Sevilla* (1990).

His photographs have also appeared in various books and group catalogs, such as *La familia europea* (1959), *Fotografía catalana de los cincuenta* (1985), *Fotógrafos de la Escuela de Madrid* (1988), *Cuatro direcciones* (1991), *75 años de fotografía Leica* (1991), and *Grupo Afal* (1991).

In 1965 he began an intensive period of work as director and producer of film documentaries, winning major awards with *El Prado vivo* and *El que enseña*. In 1966 he started working for TVE (Televisión Española), producing such series as *Conozca usted España* and *Raíces*. In 1970 he directed the film *Topical Spain*.

Most recently he has produced a number of books for the publishers Lunwerg, including *Madrid, Madrid* (1995).

MASPONS, ORIOL

Oriol Maspons Casades was born in Barcelona in 1928. In 1955 he moved to Paris, where he lived for two years. In 1956 he joined the editorial board of the magazine *Afal* and in 1957 set up a photographic studio in Barcelona. In 1962 he formed a professional partnership with Julio Ubiña.

A regular contributor to many publications, including *La Gaceta Ilustrada, Elle, L'Oeil, Paris-Match*, and *Boccaccio*, he has also worked in many different countries, producing much distinguished work in the fields of fashion, portrait, and advertising photography.

His photographs have been shown in numerous exhibitions, such as *Fotografía catalana de los años cincuenta* (1985) and *Grupo Afal* (1991). He has produced several books, among them *Toreo de salón* (1962), in collaboration with Julio Ubiña, *Poeta en Nueva York* (1965), *La caza de la perdiz roja* (1962), and *Personajes de compañía* (1995).

He is also the author of the book *Els Barcelonins* (1988), compiled in conjunction with Colita and Xavier Miserachs.

In 1995, the Fundación La Caixa organized a retrospective exhibition of his work, which also formed the subject of the book *Oriol Maspons, l'Instant perdut*.

Cristina Sanz

Ana Muller

MENCHÓN, PEDRO

Pedro Menchón Peñas was born in Lorca, Murcia, in 1897. He took up photography young, working as an assistant in José Rodrigo's studio. In the early 1920s, as Rodrigo approached retirement, he began to take his own portrait photographs and produce photoreportages.

Although it is far below Rodrigo's standard, his work has an admirable clarity, is professionally impeccable though devoid of the slightest originality. The direct and straightforward manner of his work places him in that group of popular all-purpose photographers who, although they never attained brilliance, record perfectly adequately the reality of provincial Spain; his photographs today constitute an intimate documentation of the lives of ordinary Spaniards of the period.

Like many professional photographers in the provinces, Menchón worked as a portrait and press photographer. He was a regular contributor to the regional press and to such publications as *ABC* and *Blanco y Negro*. He died in Lorca in 1955. His work is preserved in the Archivo Municipal in Lorca.

MISERACHS, XAVIER

Xavier Miserachs Ribalta was born in Barcelona in 1937. He took his first photographs at the age of 14, and in 1959 gave up medicine to become a professional photographer. In 1964 he published *Barcelona en blanc i negre*, a key work among books on Spanish photography of the postwar years. His photographs have appeared in a large number of magazines all over the world, such as *La Actualidad Española*, *Triunfo*, *Magazin*, *Paris-Match*, *Bazaar*, and *Gaceta Ilustrada*. He has also worked as an advertising photographer.

His work has been shown in numerous exhibitions, and he has been important as a teacher and writer on photography. He is the founder of the Escuela Eina, where he also taught, and is the author of a large number of articles published in such magazines as *Imagen y Sonido* and the bulletin *Afal*. He is also the author of several books, including *Costa Brava Show* (1966), *Los Cachorros* (1969), *Les altres capitals* (1987, *Catalunya a vol d'ocell* (1984), and *Els Barcelonins* (1988), compiled in conjunction with Colita and Oriol Maspons.

In 1922 the Fundación La Caixa organized an exhibition of his work, and published the catalog *Xavier Miserachs, 1 segon i 25 centesimes*. His book *Profesiones con futuro: fotógrafo* was published by Grijalbo in 1995.

MULLER, NICOLÁS

Nicolás Muller was born in Orosháza, Hungary, in 1913. He fled his country in 1938 and settled in Paris, where he worked for *France Magazine* and *Regard*. The German occupation of France forced him to move again, this time to Portugal and Tangier. In Tangier he set up as a portrait photographer and produced such books as *Estampas marroquíes* and *Tánger por el Jalifa*. He settled in Madrid in 1947.

Besides his work as a portrait photographer, Muller worked extensively as a press photographer and illustrator of books on the towns, countryside, and people of Spain; among these books are *España clara* (1966), *País Vasco* (1967), *Andalucía* (1968), and *Cantabria* (1969).

His photographs have appeared in Spanish and foreign magazines, and have been exhibited in New York, Stuttgart, Jerusalem, Tel Aviv, Buenos Aires, and Budapest. In 1965 an exhibition of his work entitled *Imágenes de una vida* toured to several Spanish cities. In 1988 his work was exhibited in his native town and in 1992 he published a selection of his photographs under the title *Recuerdo de Marruecos*.

A retrospective exhibition of his work, *Nicolás Muller, fotógrafo*, was shown in Madrid in 1994, with a lavishly illustrated catalog. He now lives in Andrín, Asturias, and is no longer active as a photographer.

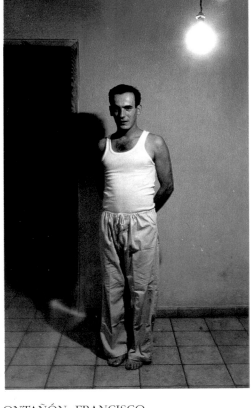

Self-portrait

OLIVÉ, JORDI

Jordi Olivé was born in Alforja, Tarragona, in 1929. A farmer by trade, he took up photography in 1957, and played an active part in the foundation of a local Agrupación Fotográfica. His work, intimately related to everyday life in Alforja, constitutes a penetrating, straightforward, and sensitive record of the life of its inhabitants. Espousing the austerity and simplicity of the great Spanish popular photographers, Olivé works without the slightest pretentiousness, producing precise images that are strongly eloquent and objective.

His work, for which he has won awards in various competitions and exhibitions, was shown by J. M. Ribas Prous in the Primavera Fotográfica in Barcelona in 1984. The same year a selection of his work was shown in the Mois de la Photo in Paris and the following year in Perpignan. Since then he has had one-man shows in several Spanish and French cities, such as Guadalajara and Orléans. His work has also appeared in various group exhibitions and catalogs, including *Tiempo de silencio. Panorama de la fotografía española de los años 50–60* (1992), and *Els nostres fotógrafs (els pioners)* (Reus, 1995).

ONTAÑÓN, FRANCISCO

Francisco Ontañón Núñez was born in Barcelona in 1930. He soon became established as an amateur photographer by joining the Asociación Fotográfica de Cataluña (1954) and the group Afal (1950).

In 1957 he moved to Madrid to take up photography professionally. Working for *Europa Press* and *La Actualidad Española*, he covered all kinds of national and international issues.

He has published several books, including *Los días iluminados* (1964), *El libro de la caza menor* (1963), *Vivir en Madrid* (1967), *Catalonia* (1970), and *Animales salvajes*. His photographs have also appeared in such specialist magazines as *Imagen y Sonido*, *Afal*, and *Arte Fotográfico*.

He has exhibited in many one-man shows and group exhibitions, among them *Fotográfos de la Escuela de Madrid* (1988), *Historia del fotoperiodisme a Catalunya, 1885–1976* (1990), and *Grupo Afal, 1956–1991* (1991). With other members of Afal he has also taken part in many exhibitions in Madrid, Barcelona, Paris, Moscow, Pescara, Cologne, Brussels, and Munich.

Since 1979 he has worked for the weekly supplement of the daily newspaper *El País*.

PATO, HERMES

Hermes Pato Velayos was born in Salamanca in 1896. He started taking photographs at the age of 17. He worked as a portrait photographer in Salamanca and Zamora, and for some years was the picture editor of the *Gaceta Regional*.

In 1937 he joined the press and propaganda department of the Nationalist movement, and was a founder of the picture agency Efe. Working as a press photographer during the Spanish Civil War, he covered various military events.

After the war he was a key organizer of the services provided by Efe, for which he worked continuously until his retirement in 1965. He was also General Franco's official photographer at El Pardo and one of the most active press photographers of the time. After the death of Miguel Cortés, he was appointed director of Cifra's photographic services.

For many years he was president of the first Asociación de Redactores Gráficos de Madrid (Indeprofo), which counted among its members press photographers with such different backgrounds as Alberto Lendiñez, Díaz Casariego, Contreras, Verdugo, Santos Yubero, and Campúa. He died in Madrid in 1978.

Joan Gaspar

Self-portrait

PÉREZ DE ROZAS, CARLOS

Carlos Pérez de Rozas y Masdéu was born in Madrid in 1894. He began working for *La Vanguardia* in Barcelona at the age of 18, but soon abandoned the pen for the camera, joining the daily newspaper *Las Noticias*.

In 1929 he was appointed official photographer for the World Fair in Barcelona. In 1930 he set up a studio in Las Ramblas, where he worked until the proclamation of the Spanish Republic. He then resumed work as a press photographer on the staff of *El Día Gráfico* and *La Noche*. After the Spanish Civil War he returned to *La Vanguardia*, where he worked until his death in 1954, which occurred as he was covering the arrival of the ship *Semiramis* in Barcelona.

With Merletti and Branguli, Pérez de Rozas was one of Barcelona's most emblematic press photographers. Like them, he also stood at the head of a major dynasty of photographers who continued, and still continue, his work. Among them are his sons Carlos, José Luis, Manuel, Enrique, and Rafael Pérez de Rozas y Sáenz de Tajada. *Els Pérez de Rozas*, a retrospective exhibition of work by the Pérez de Rozas family, was shown in Barcelona in 1994.

PÉREZ SIQUIER, CARLOS

Carlos Pérez Siquier was born in Almería in 1930. He took up photography in 1952. With José María Artero he founded and played an active part in the group Afal (1956). From 1956 to 1962 he worked as editor of Afal's bulletin and with Artero he edited Afal's 1958 yearbook and those issued by Everfoto from 1973 to 1976.

His photographs have appeared in all the leading Spanish and foreign magazines, and he has shown his work in many one-man and group exhibitions, such as those held in Charleroi, Pescara, Paris, Munich, Berlin, and Moscow (1956–62), the Galería Multitud in Madrid (1976), Rencontres internationales de la photographie in Arles (1978), Círculo de Bellas Artes de Madrid (1983), Primavera Fotográfica in Barcelona (1984), and the Musée Cantini in Marseilles (1988).

As a critic and writer on photography, he has also published a large number of articles in magazines, yearbooks, and catalogs.

In recent years he has taken part in such exhibitions as *Grupo Afal, 1956–1991* (1991), *Cuatro direcciones. Fotografía contemporánea española* (1991) and *Imatges escollides. La collecció Gabriel Cualladó* (1993).

POMÉS, LEOPOLDO

Leopoldo Pomés was born in Barcelona in 1931. He developed an interest in painting and literature at an early age, and was taking his first photographs in 1952. In 1961, with Karin Leiz, he set up Estudios Pomés, where he developed an interest in movies and in advertising photography, areas in which he quickly became established. Four years later he was awarded first prize at the Festival de Cinema Publicitaire in Cannes and in 1972 the Golden Lion at the Venice Festival. In 1982, his work, alongside that of Catalá Roca and Xavier Miserachs, was exhibited in Barcelona.

His photographs illustrate many books, among them *Las Ventanas* by R. M. Rilke (1957) and *Gaudí, arquitectura d'anticipació* by Joan Perucho (1970). He has also made several films and videos, such as *Ensalada Baudelaire* (1978), *Barcelona, Open City* (1988), *Josep Plá, viatger* (1991), and *Barcelona, una passió* (1992).

His work has appeared in various magazines, yearbooks, and catalogs, including *Everfoto, Fotografies catalanes dels anys cinquanta* (1985), and *Imatges escollides. La collecció Gabriel Cualladó* (1993).

The book *Leopoldo Pomés*, by J. M. García Ferrer and Martí Rom, was published in 1994.

Self-portrait

QUINTAS, ÁNGEL

Ángel Quintas was born in Zamora in 1931. At the age of 17 he joined the cartographic division of the Spanish air force. In 1951, after completing his studies in Seville, he moved to Barcelona, where he worked as an aerial photographer.

In Barcelona he became professionally established and in 1955 he set up a photographic studio in Zamora. His work is closely linked to the city's artistic scene and has always steered clear of the technical perfection upheld by photographic clubs of his time. On another level, Quintas has always had a special interest in experimentation with photography.

He has been a contributor to the regional illustrated press, and his photographs have been used to illustrate various cultural monographs. In 1975 he closed his studio in Zamora and settled in Vitoria. There he worked as a medical photographer until his death in 1978.

A retrospective exhibition of his work, entitled *Ángel Quintas, fotográfias. 1950–1970*, was held in 1993. The exhibition was accompanied by a fine catalog, with text by Cristina Zélich. An archive of his work is preserved at Filmoteca de Castilla y León, in Salamanca.

RIBAS PROUS, JOSEP MARÍA

Josep María Ribas Prous was born in Barcelona in 1940. He began taking photographs in 1957 and enrolled at the Agrupación Fotográfica de Reus (AFR) in 1961.

In 1975 he established the Cursos de Consulta within the AFR, and undertook the huge task of gathering together and cataloging the work of local photographers. In 1990 he oversaw the establishment of the Fototeca Histórica de Reus.

As a photographer, he stands out among his countrymen as the one who has probably won the highest number of prizes and awards. Since 1965 he has been nominated for over 1,000 awards and more than 100 international prizes, including the Moscow Exhibition (1978) and the Gran Premio Negtor (1981).

Between 1976 and 1990 he had more than 100 one-man shows in various European countries, and his work has appeared in magazines and yearbooks all over the world, including *Arte Fotográfico* (1973), *Coteflash* (1974), *Everfoto* (1973–76), *Photography Year Book* (1980), and *Foto Sovietica* (1985).

He has also edited various collections of photographs and the book *Els nostres pioners* (Reus, 1995). He is now president of the Agrupación Fotográfica de Reus.

RUEDA, JORGE

Jorge Rueda was born in Almería in 1943. Having taught himself photography, he began his career as a studio photographer. He was picture editor of the magazine *Triunfo* and contributed to Ediciones Ruedo Ibérico. In Madrid in 1971 he launched the magazine *Nueva Lente*, and was its editor from 1975 to 1979.

He is the author of several books on photography and was the founder and editor of *Aquí Imagen*. He has been a member of the selection committee for Spanish photography, and a member of the jury at the Rencontres Internationales de la Photographie in Arles (1978), as well as lecturing at various universities.

In recent years he has given many courses, tutorials, and lectures on the themes of photographic technique and esthetics, and the rearing of animals in captivity.

His work has appeared in various magazines and has been exhibited in Madrid, Rome, Berlin, Stockholm, Beijing, Tokyo, and Casasimarro. More recently his work has been chosen for exhibitions such as *Cuatro Direcciones* (1991), *Imagina* (1992), *Montpellier Photovision* (1993), and *Spanish Vision* (1992).

Self-portrait

Self-portrait

Self-portrait

SANTOS YUBERO, MARTÍN

Martín Santos Yubero was born in Madrid in 1902. In 1927 he joined the staff of the daily newspaper *La Nación* as picture editor. After the Spanish Republic had been proclaimed, he began to contribute to the major illustrated news publications of Madrid, such as *Estampa, Ahora,* and *La Crónica.*

After a brief period working on *La Luz,* he joined the editorial staff of the *Diario de Madrid* in late 1933. During the Civil War he worked for various publications and, together with the brothers Benítez Casaus, he launched a press agency that provided photographs to various publications in Spain and abroad.

After the Spanish Civil War, Santos Yubero became head of syndication on the daily newspaper *Ya,* becoming one of the unofficial photographers of the new regime. He specialized in photographs of bullfighting and in 1950 published a monograph on Manolete. He went on working right up until his death in Madrid in 1992.

His collection of over 20,000 negatives, comprising photographs taken by himself as well as by people with whom he worked, is preserved in the documents department of the Comunidad de Madrid.

SANZ LOBATO, RAFAEL

Rafael Sanz Lobato was born in Seville in 1932. In 1964 he enrolled at the Real Sociedad Fotográfica in Madrid but left a few months later. He returned in 1966, together with other photographers, among them Carlos Corcho, Sigfrido de Guzmán, Nieto Canedo, and Donato de Blas, with whom he established the group La Colmena. In 1972, with Corcho, Vila Masip, Sanchis Soler, and Juan Antonio Sáenz, he created Grupo-5. A pioneer of humanist photojournalism with an anthropological basis, Sanz Lobato is one of the most important yet most neglected photographers of the Madrid School.

His work has been shown in various group exhibitions and in a dozen one-man shows in the Sala Aixelà in Barcelona (1971) and the Fundación Colegio del Rey in Alcalá de Henares (1990). His photographs have appeared in various magazines, catalogs, and yearbooks, including *Arte Fotográfico, Imagen y Sonido, Everfoto, Coteflash, Cuatro Años de Fotografía* (Nueva Lente, 1975), and *Fotógrafos de la Escuela de Madrid* (1988). *Rafael Sanz Lobato. Fotografías,* a catalog devoted to his work, was published in 1990. His latest portrait photographs were shown in 1996 in an exhibition entitled *Rafael Lobato. Retratos.*

SCHOMMER, ALBERTO

Alberto Schommer was born in Vitoria in 1928. He developed a keen interest in photography from an early age, and in 1958 joined the group Afal. He established his first studio, in Vitoria, in 1961 and in 1966 moved to Madrid, where he worked as a portrait, advertising, and industrial photographer. In 1972 he began publishing his famous *Retratos Psicológicos* and began to produce his series *Dulce violencia, Tierra fermentada,* and *Cascografías.*

His photographs have appeared in a wide range of magazines, yearbooks, anthologies, and catalogs, including *Afal* (1991) and *Cuatro Direcciones* (1991). He has also produced numerous books, among them *Fotos Psicológicas* (1975), *El grito de un pueblo* (1978), *Euskalerría* (1987), *Retratos* (1990), *Ausencias* (1990), *La búsqueda* (1993), *El viaje* (1995), and *La vida (La Habana)* (1994).

His work has been exhibited in numerous one-man shows in such galleries as the Château d'Eau in Toulouse (1977), the Galería Juana Mordó in Madrid (1985), the Círculo de Bellas Artes de Madrid (1989), the Centre Georges Pompidou in Paris (1990), and Il Diafragma in Milan (1995).

In January 1996 he was made a member of the Real Academia de Bellas Artes of San Fernando.

Self-portrait

Self-portrait

Cualladó

TERRÉ, RICARD

Ricard Terré was born in Sant Boi de Llobregat, Barcelona, in 1928. He took up photography in 1955 and the following year his work was shown in the group exhibition *La Fotografía Española de Hoy*, at the Club Photographique in Paris. In 1958 he joined the group Afal and with other members exhibited his work in Moscow, Charleroi, Pescara, Milan, Paris, Munich, and Berlin.

In 1960 his photographs were shown in *Foto Club* in Vigo, when he took part in the group exhibition *Subjektive Photography 3*, organized by Otto Steinert. In 1964 his work was again chosen by Steinert for his book *Autorretratos en la Historia de Fotografía*. In 1991, a retrospective exhibition of his work was shown in Vigo, accompanied by a catalog, *Ricard Terré*.

His work has appeared in various Spanish and foreign magazines, including *Photo-Review, Destino, Berliner International, Afal, Imagen y Sonido*, and *Welt Ausstellung der Photographie*. His photographs have also been published in such group catalogs as *Espacios* (Vigo, 1986) and *Grupo Afal*, 1956–1991 (Almería, 1991). In 1995 the Fundación La Caixa organized a retrospective exhibition of his work, which was accompanied by the publication of a book, *Ricard Terré*.

UBIÑA, JULIO

Julio Ubiña Peña was born in Santander in 1922. Between 1936 and 1940 he lived in Paris. In 1964 he enrolled at the Agrupación Fotográfica de Cataluña and in 1957 established Barcelona's first professional color laboratory.

In 1962 he went into partnership with Oriol Maspons. As a staff member on the *Gaceta Ilustrada* and the picture agency *Rapho*, he traveled extensively abroad and took a large number of photographs. With Oriol Maspons, he produced the books *Toreo de salón* (1962) and *Poeta en Nueva York* (1965).

Between 1970 and 1978 he combined his work as a photographer with movie and television advertising. He gave up photography in 1978.

His work has appeared in various Spanish and foreign magazines, and in many one-man shows and group exhibitions, such as the one he shared with Maspons in the Sala Aixelá (1959) and the group exhibition *Fotografies catalanes dels anys cinquanta* (1985).

In 1990 the Fundació La Caixa organized a retrospective exhibition entitled *Julio Ubiña*, with photographs selected by Josep Gol.

He died in Barcelona in 1988.

VIELBA, GERARDO

Gerardo Vielba was born in Madrid in 1921. After attending drawing classes, he began taking his first photographs in 1935. In 1954 he enrolled at the Real Sociedad Fotográfica in Madrid, and became its president in 1964. He is a distinguished member of the Madrid School, and his work has appeared in various magazines, yearbooks, and catalogs, including *Arte Fotográfico, Imagen y Sonido, Afal*, and *Cuadernos de Fotografía*, on whose editorial board he served. His work has also been shown in many group exhibitions, such as those that took place in the Galería Multitud (1976) and in *Fotógrafos de la Escuela de Madrid* (1988).

He was without doubt the most prominent theorist of the Madrid School of photographers of his generation, exerting a great influence on the younger members of the Real Sociedad de Fotógrafos. He was the author of many articles and essays, the organizer of many conferences and symposia on photography, and the compiler of the book *José Ortiz Echagüe. Sus fotografías* (1978). In 1993 a retrospective exhibition of his work entitled *Gerardo Vielba, fotógrafo (1921–1992)* was shown in Madrid. The same year the Real Sociedad de Fotógrafos organized the exhibition *Homenaje a Gerardo Vielba*.

He died in Madrid in 1992.

HISTORICAL OVERVIEW

PHOTOGRAPHY	POLITICS	CULTURE AND SOCIETY
1939		
Negra i Tort resumes paper manufacture. Matutano starts making Nerva cameras. Centelles, the Mayo brothers, and other leading photojournalists leave Spain to go into exile.	End of the Spanish Civil War. Spain is expelled from the League of Nations. Outbreak of World War II The Political Responsibility Law is passed.	Ration cards are issued. The Coros y Danzas are established. The Consejo Superior de Investigaciones Científicas is founded. Antonio Machado dies in exile.
1940		
The Fundación de Productos Fotográficos *Valca* is established in Llodio. The Department of Photography is created at MOMA in New York. *Cent ans de Photographie* by Georges Potonnié is published.	In January, the number of political prisoners stands at 250,000. Julián Besteiro dies in prison; Manuel Azaña dies in exile. Lluís Companys is executed. Franco meets Hitler. Freemasonry and Communism are outlawed.	Dionisio Ridruejo launches the magazine *Escorial*. *Eloísa está debajo del almendro*, by Jardiel Poncela, is published. Celia Gámez's *Yola* is premiered. The Consejo de la Hispanidad (later the Instituto de Cultura Hispánica) is established.
1941		
The Negtor factory opens in Barcelona. Plá Janini's work is exhibited at the Galerías Laietanas.	Germany invades the Soviet Union. The Blue Division leaves for the Russian front. Death of Alfonso XIII in Rome. The United States joins World War II.	*La forja de un rebelde*, by Arturo Barea, *Entre el clavel y la espada*, by Rafael Alberti, and *Raza*, by Sáenz de Heredia, are published. Radio Pirenaica begins broadcasting from Moscow.
1942		
Matutano begins to manufacture its Perfecta and Capta-Baby cameras.	Spain and Portugal sign the Iberian Pact. Allied landings in North Africa.	*La familia de Pascual Duarte*, by C. J. Cela, is published. NO-DO is launched. Miguel Hernández dies in prison.
1943		
España mística, by Ortiz Echagüe, is published.	The Blue Division is disbanded. Mussolini falls from power. Battle of Stalingrad.	*Being and Nothingness*, by Jean-Paul Sartre, and *La fiel infantería*, by R. García Serrano, are published. The magazine *Garcilaso* is launched.
1944		
The work of Ortiz Echagüe is exhibited. The first issue of *Sombras* appears. Robert Capa photographs the Normandy landings. The work of Weegee (Arthur H. Fellig) is exhibited at MOMA in New York.	Allied landings in Normandy. Resistance groups become active in Spain. The United States declares the Spanish government undemocratic and totalitarian.	*Desde la última vuelta del camino*, by Pío Baroja, and *Nada*, by Carmen Laforet, are published. The first issue of *La Estafeta Literaria* appears. *Sombra del paraíso*, by Vicente Aleixandre, and *Hijos de la ira*, by Dámaso Alonso, are published. Penicillin comes into use in Spain.

PHOTOGRAPHY	POLITICS	CULTURE AND SOCIETY

1945

The *Grupo de los XV* is formed in Paris. The work of Paul Strand is exhibited in New York. *Histoire de la Photographie*, by Raimond Lecuyer, and *Photographs, 1915–1945*, by Paul Strand, are published.	Germany is defeated. Mussolini is captured and shot. Atomic bombs are dropped on Hiroshima and Nagasaki. Japan surrenders. The Nuremberg Trials begin. Spain's application to join the United Nations is rejected.	*Campo de sangre*, by Max Aub, is published. Death of Gutiérrez Solana, José María Sert, and Ignacio Zuloaga. José Ortega y Gasset returns to Spain.

1946

The Asociación Fotográfica de Galicia is founded in Vigo. *Orientaciones fotográficas*, by Antonio Campañá, is published. A retrospective of the work of Henri Cartier-Bresson is shown at MOMA in New York. The first issue of *Popular Photography* appears.	The United Nations ostracizes the Franco regime. Many countries cut off diplomatic relations with Spain. The Philippines gain independence. Spain establishes a trade agreement with Argentina.	The first issue of *Ínsula* appears. The group *Arte Nuevo* is formed. Manuel de Falla dies in exile. *Cementiri de Sinera*, by Salvador Espriu, is published.

1947

The group *La Bussola* is formed. *Vision in Motion*, by László Moholy-Nagy, is published. Magnum, the picture agency, is established.	The Marshall Plan is implemented. Resistance groups cease their activities. The Law of Succession is passed by Parliament. Eva Perón visits Spain.	*La sombra del ciprés es alargada*, by Miguel Delibes, is published. Death of Manuel Machado. Manolete, the bullfighter, is gored to death.

1948

Sevilla en fiestas, by Luis Arenas, and the photographic anthology *Luz y Sombras* are published. Juan Gyenes opens his studio in Madrid.	Spain is excluded from the Marshall Plan. Spain and Portugal extend the Iberian Pact. The state of Israel is established. Gandhi is assassinated.	*Viaje a la Alcarria*, by Camilo José Cela, and *Locura de amor*, by Juan de Orduña, are published. The magazine *Dau al Set* is launched in Barcelona.

1949

Otto Steinert, Peter Keetman, and Wolfgang Reisewitz establish the group *Fotoform*, in Stuttgart. *Camera in Paris*, by Brassaï, and *La banlieue de Paris*, by Robert Doisneau, are published.	NATO is formed. The king of Jordan visits Spain. The Soviet Union develops the atomic bomb. The People's Republic of China is proclaimed.	*El vencido*, by Manuel Andújar, *La casa encendida*, by Luis Rosales, and *Historia de una escalera*, by Buero Vallejo, are published. Death of Joaquín Turina. *España como problema*, by Laín Entralgo, is published.

1950

The first issue of *Photokina* appears in Cologne. *Camera in Pont Lobos*, by Edward Weston, is published. The Polaroid camera is launched. The first issue of *Camera* appears.	Spain and the Soviet Union resume diplomatic relations. Spain joins the Food and Agriculture Organization. The Korean War breaks out.	*Canto General*, by Pablo Neruda, and *Ángel fieramente humano*, by Blas de Otero, are published. Death of Alfonso Rodríguez Castelao. Rationing ends.

PHOTOGRAPHY	POLITICS	CULTURE AND SOCIETY
1951		
Subjetive Photografie, by Otto Steinert, and *Nudes*, by Martín Munckacsi, are published. The *Club 30 x 40* is formed. *PhotoLeague* is disbanded.	General strike in Barcelona. Luis Carrero Blanco becomes presidential undersecretary. The Paris Treaty takes place.	*La colmena*, by Camilo José Cela, and *Surcos*, by José Antonio Nieves Conde, are published. Pedro Salinas dies in exile.
1952		
The first issues of *Arte Fotográfico*, *Images*, and *Aperture* appear. *Images à la sauvette*, by Henri Cartier-Bresson, is published.	Spain joins UNESCO. Dwight Eisenhower is elected president of the United States. The Soviet Union develops the hydrogen bomb.	*Lo demás es silencio*, by Gabriel Celaya, and *Tres sombreros de copa*, by M. Mihura, are published. Death of Jardiel Poncela. Bread rationing ends.
1953		
Catalá Roca exhibits at the Sala Caralt. *Ballet español*, by Juan Gyenes, is published. Higinio Negra establishes the Premio Negtor.	Spain signs military and trade agreements with the United States. Death of Stalin. Spain signs the Vatican Concordat. End of the Korean War.	*Réquiem por un campesino español*, by Ramón Sender, *Los cipreses creen en Dios*, by José María Gironella, and *Escuadra hacia la muerte*, by Alfonso Sastre are published. *Bienvenido Mister Marshall*, by Luis García Berlanga, is screened.
1954		
Barcelona, by Catalá Roca, is published. The group *Misa* (Mario Giacomelli, Ferroni, Silvio Pellegrini, Piergiorgio Branzi) is formed. Death of Robert Capa and Werner Bischof. *Les Parisiens tels qu'ils sont*, by Robert Doisneau, is published.	Josep Tarradellas becomes president of the Generalitat (Catalonia's historical governing body) in exile. University students protest against the regime. The Warsaw Pact is formed.	*El fulgor y la sangre*, by Ignacio Aldecoa, and *Marcelino pan y vino*, by Ladislao Vadja, are published. Death of Jacinto Benavente. The *Semiramis* docks in Barcelona.
1955		
The Family of Man, by Edward Steichen, is exhibited. The group *Friulano per una nuova Fotografia* is formed by Italo Zannier. The picture agency Sipa Press is established. *The History of Photography*, by Helmut Gersheim, and *Les Européens*, by Henri Cartier-Bresson, are published.	Student protests cause serious disturbance. The technocrats of Opus Dei rise to power. Spain joins the United Nations.	*El balneario*, by Carmen Martín Gaite, and *Muerte de un ciclista*, by J. A. Bardem, are published. Movie conferences take place in Salamanca. Death of José Ortega y Gasset.
1956		
The first issue of *Afal* appears. *Spanien*, by Michael Wolgensinger, *New York*, by William Klein, and *Castillos y alcázares*, by José Ortiz Echagüe, are published.	Morocco gains independence. The Soviet Union invades Hungary. De-Stalinization begins in the Soviet Union. The first state of emergency is declared in Spain.	TVE (Televisión Española) starts broadcasting. Death of Pío Baroja. *El Jarama*, by Sánchez Ferlosio, and *Calle mayor*, by J. A. Bardem, are published. Juan Ramón Jiménez wins the Nobel Prize for Literature.

PHOTOGRAPHY	POLITICS	CULTURE AND SOCIETY

1957

Jordi Olivé forms the Sociedad Fotográfica de Alforja. *The Three Birds*, by Minor White, is published.	The European Economic Community is formed. The Ifni war breaks out. Spain joins the European Atomic Agency Commission.	*Gran sol*, by Ignacio Aldecoa, and *El último cuplé*, by Juan de Orduña, are published. The group *El Paso* is formed.

1958

The photographic anthology *Luz y Sombras* and *Afal's* yearbook are published. *Los Americanos*, by Robert Frank, is published in France. The exhibition *Ashtraction in Photography* is shown at MOMA in New York.	John XXIII is elected pope. A Nationalist fundamental law is passed. General de Gaulle becomes president of France. A state of emergency is declared in Asturias.	*Cancionero y romancero de ausencias*, by Miguel Hernández, and *Las afueras*, by Luis Goytisolo, are published. Death of Juan Ramón Jiménez.

1959

The group *La Palangana* is formed. *Indiens pas morts*, by Werner Bischof, Robert Frank, and P. Verger, is published.	President Eisenhower visits Spain. The Cuban Revolution triumphs. The Valle de los Caidos is officially opened. The Economic Stabilization Plan is implemented. ETA, the Basque separatist organization, is formed.	*Maribel y la extraña familia*, by M. Mihura, and *El pisito*, by Marco Ferreri, are published. The first Benidorm song festival takes place. Severo Ochoa wins the Nobel Prize for Medicine. Federico Martín Bahamontes wins the Tour de France.

1960

The exhibition *The Sense of Abstraction* is shown at MOMA in New York. Negra starts to manufacture photographic paper.	John F. Kennedy is elected president of the United States. Basque priests demonstrate against repression.	*Las meninas*, by Antonio Buero Vallejo, and *20 años de poesía española*, by J. M. Castellet, are published. Death of Gregorio Marañón.

1961

Perspective of Nudes, by Bill Brandt, *Libro de juegos para los niños*, by Jaime Buesa, and *Guía del rastro*, by Carlos Saura, are published.	The Berlin Wall goes up. The Spanish army withdraws from Morocco. Students and workers protest. FUDE is established.	*La calle de Valverde*, by Max Aub, is published. *Viridiana*, by Luis Buñuel, wins the Palme d'Or at the Cannes Film Festival. *Plácido*, by Luis García Berlanga, is screened. The Beatles release their first record. Ernest Hemingway commits suicide.

1962

Neutral Corner, by Ramón Masats, is published. The work of José Ortiz Echagüe is exhibited at the Biblioteca Nacional, Madrid. *Creative Photography*, by Helmut Gersheim, is published.	Vatican Council II takes place. The Cuban missile crisis breaks out. Communist labor unions form in Spain. A state of emergency is declared in Spain.	Death of Ramón Pérez de Ayala. *Longa noite de pedra*, by Celso E. Ferreiro, *Tiempo de silencio*, by Luis Martín Santos, *Tormenta de verano*, by Juan García Hortelano, and *Escrito en España*, by Dionisio Ridruejo, are published.

PHOTOGRAPHY	POLITICS	CULTURE AND SOCIETY
1963		
The first issue of *Imagen y Sonido* appears. *Los sanfermines*, by Ramón Masats, *Portrait of Myself*, by Margaret Bourke-White, *Toreo de salón*, by Oriol Maspons and Julio Ubiña, and *La caza de la perdiz roja*, by Oriol Maspons, are published.	President Kennedy is assassinated. Death of Pope John XXIII. 102 intellectuals protest against torture in Asturias. The Abbot of Montserrat is expelled from Spain. The Public Order Tribunal is set up in Spain.	Death of Ramón Gómez de la Serna and Luis Cernuda. *El verdugo*, by Luis Berlanga, is screened. The number of television owners in Spain reaches 60,000. The first issue of *Cuardernos para el diálogo* appears.
1964		
Izas, rabizas y colipoterras, by Joan Colom, *Barcelona en blanc i negre*, by Xavier Miserachs, *Moscow and Tokyo*, by William Klein, *Images of War*, by Robert Capa, and *Viejas historias de Castilla la Vieja*, by Ramón Masats, are published.	The first Development Plan is implemented. "25 years of peace" are marked. Students hold mass meetings. ETA breaks away from PNV (Partido Nacionalista Vasco).	Death of Luis Martín Santos. *Que trata de España*, by Blas de Otero, is published. *Estampa Popular* is exhibited in Valencia.
1965		
Los días iluminados, by Francisco Ontañón, and *Nuevas escenas matritenses*, by Enrique Palazuelo, are published.	SEU is disbanded. Gibraltar's sovereignty is disputed. Academics are expelled from Madrid University.	The number of television owners in Spain reaches 1,200,000. *Anatomía del realismo*, by Alfonso Sastre, is published. El Lute (Eleuterio Sánchez) is condemned to death.
1966		
The International Center for Photography opens in New York. *Costa Brava Show* and *Los cachorros*, by Xavier Miserachs, *Guía de Barcelona*, by Eugenio Forcano, and *Vivir en Madrid*, by Francisco Ontañón, are published.	The Fraga Law on press freedom is passed. A referendum on the State Organic Law is held. The Social Security Law is passed. Priests demonstrate in Barcelona.	*Señas de identidad*, by Juan Goytisolo, *Últimas tardes con Teresa*, by Juan Marsé, and *Nueve cartas a Berta*, by Basilio Martín Patino, are published. The theater company *Los Goliardos* is formed.
1967		
The magazine *Photo* is launched in Paris. The picture agency Gamma is established. *The American Way of Life*, by Josep Renau, is published.	Death of Che Guevara. Luis Carrero Blanco becomes vice-president. The border with Gibraltar is closed.	*Cien años de soledad*, by Gabriel García Márquez, and *Cinco horas con Mario*, by Miguel Delibes, are published. Death of Azorín (José Martínez Ruiz).
1968		
A retrospective of the work of Cecil Beaton is shown in London. *Libro del mar*, by Català Roca, and *Pagarse los novillos*, by García Ferrada, are published.	ETA claims its first victim. The Paris students' revolt. Prague Spring. Richard Nixon is elected president of the United States. Equatorial Guinea gains independence from Spain.	*El marxismo como moral*, by L. L. Aranguren, and *Volverás a Región*, by Juan Benet, are published. Death of León Felipe. Massiel wins the Eurovision Song Contest with *"La, La, La."*

PHOTOGRAPHY	POLITICS	CULTURE AND SOCIETY
1969		
The Carnet de Empresa Responsable is established. The first issue of *Creative Camera* appears in London. *Festa major*, by Eugenio Forcano, is published.	A three-month state of emergency is declared. Intellectuals demonstrate against torture and repression.	Death of Ignacio Aldecoa and Vázquez Díaz. The first American astronaut walks on the moon.
1970		
Exposición Mundial de Fotografía is shown at the Biblioteca Nacional, Madrid. The first Rencontres Internationales de la Photographie are held in Arles. The Galería Redor opens.	Death of General de Gaulle. New trade agreements are drawn up between Spain and the United States. The Burgos Trial takes place. Salvador Allende becomes president of Chile.	The theater company Tábano presents *Castañuela-70.* El Lute (Eleuterio Sánchez) escapes from prison in Puerto de Santa María. A General Education Law is passed.
1971		
The first issue of *Nueva Lente* appears. A permanent photography gallery opens at the Bibliothèque Nationale in Paris.	The third Development Plan is implemented. A state of emergency is declared in Guipúzcoa. Spain seeks membership of NATO.	*Canciones para después de una guerra* is censored. Pau Casals composes an anthem for the United Nations.
1972		
The first issue of *Cuadernos de Fotografía* appears. The picture agency Viva is established in Paris. The exhibition *From Today the Painting is Dead* is shown. The Instituto Provincial de Estudios Fotográficos is established in Barcelona.	The Watergate scandal breaks. Trade agreements are reached between Spain and the Soviet Union. Three workers are killed in disturbances.	Death of Max Aub. Bobby Fischer wins the world chess championship.
1973		
The *Everfoto, Spafoto,* and *Coteflash* annuals appear. Death of Gabriel Querol y Anglada. The picture agency Sigma opens in Paris. The Spectrum Gallery opens.	Luis Carrero Blanco is murdered. A military coup takes place in Chile. Death of President Allende. The 1001 Trial opens.	Death of Pablo Neruda. *El espíritu de la colmena*, by Victor Erice, is published. Death of Pablo Picasso and Pau Casals.
1974		
Prices for photographs by Alfred Stieglitz reach $4,500. The first issue of *Flash Foto* appears. Photocentro opens in Madrid.	Puig Antich is executed. Franco cedes power to Juan Carlos. The Carnation Revolution takes place in Portugal. Death of Juan Perón. The Democratic Junta is established. A state of emergency is declared in Biscay and Guipúzcoa.	The magazine *Zona Abierta* is launched. *La fundación*, by A. Bueno Vallejo, and *La prima Angélica*, by Carlo Saura, are published. The first Spanish satellite goes into orbit.
1975		
The work of David Hamilton is shown in Barcelona. *Fotos psicológicas*, by Alberto Schommer, are published. *Contrejour* is launched in Paris. The first issues of *Eikonos* and *Anófeles* appear. The groups F8 and Yeti are formed.	Death of Franco. Juan Carlos is crowned King of Spain. Green March in the Sahara. Five members of ETA and FRAP are executed. A democratic government is formed.	*Tiempo de destrucción*, by Martín Santos, and *Furtivos*, by J. L. Boráu, are published. The theater company La Cuadra presents *Quejío.* The Fundación Miró is set up. The Museo Español de Arte Contemporáneo opens.

INDEX

Lunwerg Editores would like to thank all those authors and photographers who have generously contributed to the publication of this book. Thanks are also due to the following:

Biblioteca Nacional de Madrid
Archivo Municipal de Lorca
Institut d'Estudits Fotogràfics de Catalunya
Centro Nacional de Arte Reina Sofia
Institut Municipal d'Història de Barcelona
Real Sociedad Fotográfica de Madrid
Agrupación Fotográfica de Córdoba
Agrupación Fotográfica de Guadalajara
Agrupación Fotográfica deReus
Agrupación Fotográfica de Zaragoza
Agrupación Fotográfica de Cataluña
Monte de Piedad y Caja de Ahorros de Sevilla
ABC (Madrid and Seville)
Fundación Sevillana de Electricidad
Hemeroteca Municipal de Sevilla
Hemeroteca Municipal de Madrid
Universidad de Navarra
Museo de Navarra
Ayuntamiento de Vigo
Efe
Europa Press
Archivo Municipal de Vitoria
Filmoteca de Castilla-León
Instituto Valenciano de Arte Moderno
Archivo Regional de la Comunidad de Madrid
Obra Cultural Caixa de Tarragona
Mauthausen Association
Centro de Estudios Fotográficos de Vigo
Galería Fotográfica Visor
Archivo Central de la Administración
Botán picture agency
Zardoya picture agency
Magnum
Arxiu Fotogràfic de Catalunya